Free and cheap resources for schools:

a survey and guide

Robert S Mason

The Library Association · London

14388

First published 1984

British Library Cataloguing in Publication Data
Mason, Robert S.
    Free and cheap resources for schools.
    1. School libraries——Great Britain——Administration
    I. Title
    025.1'978'0941   Z675.S3

ISBN 0 85365 886 2

To Margaret, Robert and Jamie

Designed by Geoff Green
Typeset by Library Association Publishing in 10/12pt
Rockwell/Paladium

123458887868584

Contents

1 INTRODUCTION   5

2 TYPES OF MATERIALS   15
   Books, pamphlets, leaflets, worksheets, periodicals,
   wallcharts, posters, maps, postcards, films, kits and
   samples, speakers

3 SOURCES OF MATERIALS   21
   Central government, Government supported
   agencies, Local government and public utilities,
   Teachers' professional associations, Professional and
   similar groups, Charitable organizations, Special
   interest and pressure groups, Embassies and tourist
   offices, Nationalized industries, Industrial firms.
   Currency of low-cost resources

4 SUBJECT AREAS   30
   Art   30
   Business Studies, Commerce, Economics and Money
      Management   37
   Careers   46
   Environmental Studies   56
   General Studies and Contemporary Problems   68
   Geography   74
   History   85
   Home Economics   90
   Modern Languages: French and German   96
   Physical Education   97
   Religious Education   100
   Rural Studies   103
   Science   109
   Technical Studies   119

5 CONCLUSION   126

BIBLIOGRAPHY   131

APPENDICES
    1   Books providing addresses of major firms,
         organizations, and institutions   135
    2   Sources of information about low-cost and free
         material   137
    3   Free and low-cost periodicals   142
    4   Sources of free 16mm films   146

INDEX   151

Acknowledgment

I am deeply indebted to Sheila Ray BA FLA MPhil, who guided me through my Fellowship thesis on which this book is based.

1
Introduction

Inflation, a restricted budget and yet more calls on resources make the job of the school librarian harder and more demanding as term succeeds term. From a peak in 1973[1] the purchasing power of book allowances has been declining each year to the point when it was identified that in the first nine months of 1980 the total number of school books bought had dropped by four million compared with the same period in 1979.[2] Articles in the national press on the subject over this period make harrowing reading, though it was not until 1977,[3] when the financial trend was clearly established, that they began to appear in earnest, followed in 1978 with substantial evidence in the Educational Publishers Council's *Lucky Child? Unlucky Child?*[4] which noted that not only in the past 10 years had the average price of books risen by 100%, while education authorities' expenditure had remained static, but spending varied widely between different authorities.

By 1979 the National Book League was examining the problem in detail and, in a typical sample of what books could be bought by the average school on the figures available, came to the conclusion that there were 'inadequate spending levels' and alarm should be felt 'at the implications for book provision and learning in schools'.[5]

The situation was such that school libraries came under the spotlight of the Department of Education and Science in 1980, and it was revealed that

> Regular surveys of the state of libraries in secondary schools—the subject of much criticism in recent reports—are to be carried out by the Department of Education and Science and the results published.[6]

The first survey's findings, though not published separately were implicit in the Department's *Aspects of Secondary Education in England*, appearing in December, 1979, which commented that many schools seemed to be insufficiently supplied with books.[7]

This was in fact substantiated over a year later when it was revealed in a Department of Education and Science statistics bulletin that most schools spent only £1 per head annually on library books.[8] Even the top rate of £2.50 per head found in the survey falls far short of the £4 recommended by the Working Party convened by the National Book League in 1979, and inflation has taken its toll since then.

The public library section has fared no better. A survey conducted by the National Book League in 1983 found that nationally, spending on library books had fallen by 19% cent in England and Wales since 1978/79 and that some local authorities had cut spending by up to 92%.[9]

Looking ahead, there seems little hope of improvement as expenditure on secondary education will still be declining to the extent of £80 million over the period 1981—4,[10] according to government figures. Despite the fact that the Education Secretary says that '2% compound'[11] has been earmarked for books within this term, taking into account inflation and even a dip in the number of pupils, it is forecast that the current spending figure of £51 million a year will be reduced to £44 million, and only two books would be purchased for each child, as opposed to the present four books.[12]

Over-pessimistic as it may sound, this is being borne out with figures released by the Educational Publishers Council and British Educational Equipment Association which showed in a report published in January 1983 that for 1981—2 only 19 out of the 104 authorities in England and Wales were spending at or above 1978—9 levels in secondary schools.[13]

They had already identified in the previous year 2,700 stories in the national and local press, many of which were deeply critical of the way spending on school books had been neglected,[14] as well as the fact that only the ILEA was spending more than the National Book League's 'reasonable' level of £14.27 per head a year and many authorities not even one third of this amount.[15] It is interesting to note that out of the local education finance 'cake' only 0.7% is spent on books.[16] The corollary of this is that when economies are required it is the capitation allowance which is first to be reduced and as the reductions are proportionately greater than the cuts in the education budget books suffer at an excessively high rate.

The standard of service now expected means that if the library is to remain credible, fresh initiatives will be required in the forms of service offered. More than ever it is time for taking stock of the library's objectives, reassessing priorities and defining needs, and spending more wisely with a view to what is available and what is required. In terms of resources, this is not an easy task. As a noted educationalist, Professor Wragg, in an article in *The Guardian* in January 1979 said, 'no individual can possibly know all the curriculum materials available in the field'.[17]

With a broadening of the curriculum, text books have become less important and subordinated to various other kinds of materials, especially television and its video counterparts, while, in many cases, teachers have produced their own resources or relied on project work, making the most of materials closest to hand, perhaps from the school or local library, the school library service or, it may be said, by relying on the pupils themselves to bring their own books.

The fact that an estimated 200 million illegal photocopies are taken each year perhaps reflects the situation.[18]

Ready-made packages are expensive and even the use of projectors and radio cassettes is not always possible in a school for one reason or another—the main one being that they have never been bought in sufficient quantity to be available to all potential users at any one time. Harold Peel, in his aptly named article 'A survival kit for teaching geography in a resources desert', deals with this problem in a very practical way, showing the do-it-yourself techniques and aids which a teacher can turn to when there is a lack of either hard- or software.[19]

Access to basic information is a necessity for staff and pupils, and this has been reflected in the growth of the library resource centre. In schools where the library resource centre has developed out of the needs of the school, the learning rather than the teaching aspect of education is to the fore and education is pupil-centred, and even where it is not school policy to pursue such an aim, opting for a closely-defined curriculum, based wherever possible on text books, it is still necessary to provide a wide range of material for certain Certificate of Secondary Education and General Certificate of Education courses where individual pupils are required to undertake projects.

Simultaneously, with this new approach in education and, perhaps contributing to it, a more open society has developed. Michael Young writing in 1965 was well aware of forces operating which demanded changes in the education system. He isolated three main factors that have combined together to affect traditionally held views about how education should be carried out. These factors were:

1. The population explosion.
2. The knowledge explosion.
3. The egalitarian influence.

All these changes were, he maintained, rapidly leading to the adoption of new techniques which would, in their turn, inevitably transform not merely the traditional framework of education but its content too.[20]

Over the last decade the necessity of keeping people informed has become a priority. Not only have public relations departments mush-roomed within organizations, but new societies and groups, charitable (these alone have more than £5,000 million at their disposal) and otherwise, reflecting current thought, have sprung up, themselves organs of the media, to disseminate ideas, beliefs, and specific fact, much of which is applicable to the expanded school curriculum. Topics such as modern problems, general studies, civics, environmental education, racial and sex equality, consumer education, careers and much of the Mode 3 Certificate of Secondary Education History and Geography project work are catered for in materials ranging from leaflets to films, often from primary sources in the field (yet rarely appearing in the *British National Bibliography*), at minimal cost and often free. The possibilities of this type of material have been gaining ground amongst librarians, all the more so as the economic climate has hardened, though teachers have been made aware of them through the help of such admirable publications as *Treasure Chest for Teachers*, published by the National Union of Teachers in 1960 and continuously in print ever since in revised editions, the *Source Book for Agriculture Education* of Moray House College of Education (1966), *A Source Book of Visual Aids Materials for the Teaching of Commerce*, put together by the Southern Regional Council for Further Education (1967) and *Useful Addresses for Science Teachers* (1968).

In December 1978, Rosemary Raddon, the library organizer for the Inner London Education Authority, clearly identified a wide range of free and low-cost materials. After discussing the problem of assessing the 'vast flood of material pouring off the presses' she goes on to say that

> ...societies concerned with current issues, such as Shelter and Age Concern, produce books, packs and other items of information which are invaluable in a school library...other materials can also be obtained gratis, to be discarded if unsuitable, by writing to embassies, the nationalized industries, banks, manufacturers, marketing boards and so on, many of whom produce excellent materials in the shape of charts, samples, booklets and film strips.[21]

This theme, seen against the background of the 'money drought which has inhibited the sustained growth of school libraries' by Jennifer Brice in the following year, can best be summed up in her words in that

> strategies must therefore be employed to offset present disadvantages...many firms have their own education department which produce high quality material to give away on request, and often loan films free of charge.[22]

Barbara Beswick, in *Education Libraries Bulletin*, Spring, 1980, speaking from recent experience on library provision for sixth forms in a rural comprehensive, says that she obtained

> as much material as possible for the library resources collection from a wide variety of organizations.[23]

The value of materials, however ephemeral, from newspapers and colour supplements is also highlighted in the article. This is substantiated by Nigel Richardson who has this to say on the subject:

> Text book grants are usually inadequate, and the British Press is arguably the best in the world. It is, therefore, surprising that newspapers are not more systematically exploited by teachers.[24]

Community information shares common ground with the needs of the school library, and here there is growing interest in the use of low-cost material, not only because it is cheap, but because it can prove invaluable. The British Library funded *Community Information Project* [25] pinpointed a wealth of valuable fugitive material which, being ephemeral in format, never reached the *British National Bibliography* or *The Bookseller*, a point frequently stressed in the Community Information article of the *New Library World* which often unearths valuable and interesting items: the value of leaflets, one of the most common type of low-cost materials, and of particular relevance to students, has been emphasized by Stephen Thorpe. He pointed out that

> Their main advantage over other printed materials is that they explain subjects briefly and more simply and, in this ever complex world, condensed information is at a premium. Being colourful and well designed, they are eye-catching and are certain to be used if well displayed. They are advertisements in the broadcast sense of bringing some otherwise unknown information to people's attention.[26]

The role of this information should increase if schools adopt the ideas formulated in the British Library *The Need to Know* project,[27] which is concerned with community information, and also those put forward by N Longworth in his thesis, *Information in the Secondary School Curricula*,[28] which is on a similar theme.

The value of low-cost materials, with particular relevance to companies and commercial organizations, has been recognized by *The Understanding British Industry (UBI) Project*, funded initially by the Confederation of British Industry and later by local authorities and Municipal Chamber of Commerce groups. The aim of this project has been to make teachers and their pupils more aware of the role which industry and commerce play in the economic and social life of the country. To fulfil this aim, regional resource centres and liaison officers have been created, numbering 20 by March 1981. Information has been disseminated about materials which are available:

> These materials are often produced drawing on the expertise which a company has in a particular field and are therefore authoritative on matters of techniques or processes used...and range from the provision of speakers through films to wallcharts and booklets.[29]

These publications often have long print runs, 150,000 copies having been noted for the brochure *The Claymore Story* of Occidental Oil, no doubt exceeded by others. Altogether, this material has a great potential in the school. In the Department of Education and Science's *School Curriculum*,[30] published in March 1981, it is stressed that the curriculum needs to be related to the world outside school with pupils being given a better understanding of the economic base of society and the importance to Britain of the wealth-creating process.

Similarly, in a time of financial restraint which is not expected to alter in the foreseeable future, it has seem apposite in some quarters to take stock of all existing resources on a regional basis. The Council for Educational Technology with its project initiated in 1979/80, *The Regional Co-ordination of Educational Technology Arrangements*, provides a good example which involves the three East Anglian counties and three of the Northern Home counties—Bedfordshire, Buckingham-shire and Hertfordshire. In the words of one of the key figures in the project, Derick Last, they had to

> make known the very wide range of existing regional bodies like health and water authorities, associations and professional organizations of various kinds, all of whom almost continuously have something to contribute to the work of education and who occasionally seek out ways of involving themselves.[31]

From this project, a joint catalogue of resources materialized, and a series of resources newspapers was born, each with a circulation of five thousand.

Finally another interesting side light on the usefulness of less conventional material is through research being carried out on non-official statistical sources and their role in business information. Several thousand organizations considered to be likely producers of statistical publications were contacted. These included trade associations, stockbrokers, local authorities, market and economic research organizations, academic institutions, banks, trade unions, online services and companies. The principal types of material include market research reports, house journals and trade literature, all of which suffer from lack of bibliographic control and availability. The general feeling is that such material is an untapped resource and has in some cases perhaps, more to offer than its official counterparts.[32]

It has been my aim to draw together and evaluate all these likely sources of information in order to provide an overall picture of their potential use.

The most appropriate method for accomplishing this was found to be in the form of a survey which would act as a guide, not only identifying and commenting upon specific current items and sources, but aiming to pinpoint other likely sources of production, thus providing a more rounded assessment and perhaps an insight into the philosophy of low-cost material. One of the problems with this material is that new items are constantly being issued, whilst many do not have specific names or an author by which to identify them, and even dates of publication are lacking in many instances; such deficiencies make it difficult to compile a bibliography.

It is very important that the material should be up to date and, of course, available, and whilst in practice this is one of the major strengths of low-cost items, it does mean that it may quickly be superseded or discontinued as being no longer of relevance.

There is too always the possibility that hitherto reliable sources of low-cost material may cease to operate as such or have their services curtailed. No guarantee can be given for any source, but looking back as far as 1973 to when I first began to take an interest in this material, the trend has been towards a growth in new sources, with the volume of services of existing ones remaining fairly static, the only proviso being that some organizations now charge for their services, no doubt encouraged to do so by the wide interest shown in them!

The background and substance of this book is taken from my Fellowship thesis for the Library Association. It is based on 10 years of practical experience in secondary schools when I evolved a pragmatic approach to dealing with pupils' and teachers' enquiries, in part generated by a dwindling book fund but more especially by an innate curiosity to see what was available from further afield and from what I considered primary sources. This would take the form usually of a hastily handwritten letter requesting information, written on an ad hoc basis at the instigation of an enquiry.

On this practical aspect of the subject a glimpse at an article that appeared in *Where* magazine could prove invaluable.[33] A set of guidelines is laid down which it is worth adhering to when requesting information from charities and other 'shoestring' organizations.

A follow-up to this is to refer to books written with children in mind such as *Free Stuff for Kids* (Exley Publications) and Gundrey's *250 More Things to Send Off For*, which actively encourage letter writing.

The definition of 'low-cost' has been taken as a maximum of around £2 which would include any return postage and packing if, in fact, this cost was ever mentioned.

Materials such as film strips, overhead transparencies and slides have not been included to any great extent as these, when required, have generally been available from the local authority schools library service. In any case these are not generally available free, large museums and art galleries being the only major source for loan purposes. The same cannot be said of 16mm films and their video cassette counterpart, an exceedingly useful resource, and I make no excuse for emphasizing those available.

As a number of subjects cover the same ground, it has been thought best to include certain topics (especially those in the area of environmental and general studies and agriculture) under the most relevant heading, and not to repeat details elsewhere; it is intended that the index will compensate for any deficiencies in this direction.

It is also of value at this stage to make some general comments on how the library can be more cost effective in regard to certain services and resource acquisitions.

Firstly, most societies, associations and organizations, especially those representing teachers, issue annotated lists, bibliographies, subject lists or details of other helpful organizations which enable the librarian to select books which are the best value for money. Specialist bookshops are also helpful here, such as Campaign Books[34] or Grassroots Books,[35] the former with a vast range of books, pamphlets and packs produced by voluntary groups, community groups, pressure groups and small presses. 1,000 titles are listed by topic in its two catalogues, covering such controversial issues as race, environment, transport and technology collected from over 300 publishers.

In the same vein it is worth noting two articles that appeared in *Librarians for Social Change*. The first[36] is on the subject of provision of alternative materials in libraries whilst the second[37] deals with a directory of alternative information sources—bookshops, publishers and periodicals.

The value of building up strong links with organizations in the locality of the school such as teachers' centres, specific council departments like Industrial Development and Planning Offices, Tourist Boards and public relations departments of firms cannot be over-emphasized. Then there are, of course, libraries themselves, with the local authority's schools library service heading the list. Details of these libraries and their services should be given publicity within the school and individuals, when relevant, made aware of how they can be helped, though as Barbara Beswick has said:

> the privilege of using, even for reference, the libraries of other education institutions, is not given lightly to sixth and seventh year school students.

This point must be emphasized, as must her other observation on the maximizing of resources available in higher education establishments with attention being paid to

> the possibility of a wider network of inter-institutional co-operation to improve library services to senior school students.[38]

The information demanded by the 'A' level student increasingly requires academic texts (other than set books) that are way beyond the financial capability of the school. Whilst low-cost material can be invaluable in some areas of the curriculum there is still no substitute for appropriate books.

REFERENCES

1   Educational Publishers Council. *Publishing for Schools*, 1977. 54.
2   *The Guardian*, 6 March, 1981. 11.
3   Those articles in *The Times Educational Supplement*, 3528, 18 November, 1977, and 3259, 25 November, 1977, 10-11, have perhaps the most impact. The librarian is quoted as having £300 for the financial year 1977—8 with which to buy all books, periodicals, etc for 1,860 pupils.
4   Educational Publishers Council. *Lucky Child? Unlucky Child?*, 1978.
5   National Book League. *Books for Schools*, 1978. 40.
6   *The Times Educational Supplement*, 9 May, 1980. 3.
7   *Aspects of Secondary Education in England: a survey by HM Inspectors of Schools*. HMSO, 1979.
8   Department of Education and Science. Bulletin, May 1981. (Ref 7/81). A summary of the relevant points are discussed by Owen Surridge in his article 'Books with a limited shelf life' in the *Guardian*, 2 June, 1981, 11 and Peter Matthews in 'The Appalling State of School Libraries—According to the DES'. *School Librarian* 29 (4), December 1981. 294-6.
9   Durham, Mike 'Libraries in decline because of cuts'. *The Times Educational Supplement*, 7 October, 1983. 13.
10 *Education* 159 (11), 13 March, 1981. 232.
11 Ibid.
12 *Library Association Record* 82 (7), July 1980. 305.
13 *The Teacher*, 4 February 1983. 11.
14 *The Teacher*, 25 June 1982. 16.
15 *The Teacher*, 30 April 1982. 6.
16 *Department of Education and Science Statistics Bulletin* 10/83.
17 Wragg, Prof E C 'Superteach and the Dinosaurs'. (The radical development of teaching tactics from 1960 onwards). *The Guardian*, 9 January 1979. 9.

18   *The Teacher*, 8 April 1983. 2.

19   Peel, Harold   'A survival kit for teaching geography in a resources desert'; *Teaching Geography* 3 (3) January 1978. 132-3.

20   Young, M   *Innovation and Research in Education*. Routledge and Kegan Paul, 1965. 8.

21   Raddon, Rosemary   'Stocking a school library'. *School Librarian* 26 (4) December, 1978. 316.

22   Brice, Jennifer   'School librarianship'. *New Library World* 80 (946) April, 1979. 69.

23   Beswick, Barbara   'Library provision for sixth and seventh year students in a rural comprehensive school'. *Education Libraries Bulletin* 23 (1) Spring 1980. 18-19.

24   Richardson, Nigel   'Feature probe is a classroom winner'. *The Times Educational Supplement*, 13 October 1978. 28.

25   Morby, G   *Knowhow: a guide to information, training and campaigning materials for information and advice workers. The Community Information Project*. British Library Research and Development Publications, 1979.

26   Thorpe, Stephen   'Leaflets and libraries'. *New Library World* 80 (947) May 1979. 86-7.

27   Brake, Terence   *The Need to Know: teaching the importance of information*. (Report no 5511). British Library Research and Development Department, 1980.

28   Longworth, N   *Information in the Secondary School Curricula*. M Phil thesis. Southampton University, 1976. (Unpublished).

29   Understanding British Industry Resource Centre. *Teaching Materials*, 1977. 1.

30   Department of Education and Science *The School Curriculum*, HMSO 1981.

31   Last, Derick   'Fairer distribution'. *The Times Educational Supplement* 29 May 1981. 35.

32   King, David   'Market Research Reports, house journals and trade literature'. *Aslib Proceedings* 34 (10/12) November/December 1982. 466-72.

33   *Where*, May 1981. The article was reviewed by Rick Rogers in the *Guardian* 12 June 1981. 11.

34   Campaign Books, West Library, Bridgeman Road, Islington, London N1.

35   Grassroots Books, 1 Newton Street, Piccadilly, Manchester M1 1HW.

36   *Librarians for Social Change* Vol 8 (PO Box 450, Brighton BN1 8GR).

37   *Librarians for Social Change* Vol 22.

38   Beswick, Barbara   'Library provision for sixth and seventh year students in a rural comprehensive school'. *Education Libraries Bulletin* 23 (1) Spring 1980. 20-1.

2
Types of materials

The resources which may be obtained either free or at low-cost range widely from books and pamphlets through periodicals, posters, maps, films and samples to speakers. In some cases the material may prove to be unique, as well as the most authoritative information on the subject.

Before examining the various types of materials it is worth looking at resources which may be available in and around the school from pupils, parents and staff. Such resources could include all the national newspapers including the Sunday colour supplements (those unsold are usually available from the local newsagent by the bundle), magazines and illustrative material such as firms' brochures (especially on subjects like cars, lorries, motorcycles and fishing which pupils collect but eventually lose interest in), and calendars. Individual articles and illustrations can be extracted and mounted, if required, to be filed away for reference.

The important point when daily and weekly periodicals are being used as resource material is that the supply, albeit slightly out of date, although preferably no more than one week, should be regular and reliable. This is a case where the librarian must build up strong personal links with those responsible for donations.

Books

Printed material in substantial book form is available free but is by no means common. These one-off sporadic specimens are invariably reviewed in *The Times Educational Supplement* or the *Teacher*, as their content will be of value to some aspect of education, and perhaps of relevance to a member of staff in the school: a sourcebook on international understanding[1] from the Department of Education and Science; an Independent Broadcasting Authority report entitled

Curriculum Decision-making and Educational Television;[2] Shell's *Energy to Use or Abuse*,[3] a useful background book for sixth form economics students; the *Soviet Worker, Illusions and Realities*,[4] a selection of essays by experts on Soviet society from the information department of NATO; and *Singapore '82*,[5] a substantial hardback book detailing most aspects of the state from the country's High Commission in London.

Pamphlets

The scope of these is enormous, and their value for project work, especially where the less academic are concerned, cannot be over-stated. Information in them is usually current and backed up by statistics where necessary, the text is succinct, often providing the best introduction to the subject in question, and, above all, is supplemented with excellent colour illustrations and diagrams. Examples include *A First Look at Oil* by the Institute of Petroleum, *The Story of British Insurance*, the Polytechnic of North London's *Semi Conductors and the Silicon Chip* and the Commission for Racial Equality's *Ethnic Minorities in Britain*. Their size is such that they can be retained by the student within his folder for the duration of the project, providing a handy ready reference, without detriment to the library's bookstock which can always be referred to when the class is working in the library. This highlights one of the problems faced by the library, the necessity of providing material for a number of classes, all the members of which are pursuing different topics. The use of pamphlet material can, to some extent, ameliorate the position. One major area where it is certainly of value is in Certificate of Secondary Education Geography, a point to be covered later, but suffice it to say at this stage that pamphlet type material can provide the key to a host of subjects—sheep farming, rubber, timber production, national parks, beverages, agricultural products and coal, to name but a few.

Leaflets

Again, a wide range of information is available in this form with particular emphasis on subjects such as careers, home economics, and those general interest topics like motorcycles, guns, lorries, football, cars, aircraft and pets. This material is ideal for stimulating pupils' interests, and encouraging them to put their literary skills to practical use by writing letters to firms for information on their hobbies and sports.

On a more academic level, leaflets, often in multiple copies, can provide invaluable information on the purposes and services of major institutions and organizations which have relevance to education such as the British Standards Institution, the Office of Fair Trading and the British Road Federation.

Types of materials

Worksheets

Multiple copies of material designed first and foremost as worksheets for pupils to complete, as well as forms and documents which can be used as such for practical purposes, are available. In the first category are examples such as the Post Office's series on *The History of the Mail* and the North West Water Authority's *Life Cycle of Water* programme. Within the second category are tax forms and various financial documents—cheques, hire purchase agreements and the like. Generally this material is aimed at the less academic pupil in the fifth form.

Periodicals

Periodicals, a full list of which is given in Appendix 3, ranging from formal journals such as *Atom* from the United Kingdom Atomic Energy Authority or *British Telecom Journal* to popular magazines or newspaper-type presentations such as *Ford News* and *Employment News* are often distributed free. These periodicals are usually well produced, on good quality paper, with clear type and illustrated in both black and white and colour. A long run of the more formal type of periodical such as *Esso Magazine, Europe '82* or the *Midland Bank Reviews* build up into a substantial amount of information, and these are often indexed annually by the producing authority.

They cover fairly extensively the fields of technology, communications, transport and finance with information that is not only current but compiled from primary sources such as government departments (the Treasury or the Department of Employment), international bodies (North Atlantic Treaty Organization or the European Community), or multinational industries such as Shell. The fact that this kind of information is available in short articles increases its use as periodicals well displayed are often read not only by conscientious students but by those browsing, who may alight on something which was at first thought uninteresting.

Wallcharts

These, as distinct from posters (to be dealt with next), convey useful information and invariably combine the quality of being attractive with that of being instructive. Most topics are represented by this material be they scientific—*The Hydrological System* (National Water Council) or *Satellite Communication* (British Telecom); financial—*Money in the Community* (Midland Bank) or *Money Saving and Investment* (Bank Education Service) or simply of general interest with an example such as the BBC/Daily Mirror's *Love and Sex—feelings in relationships* and *You and Your Rights*. All have explanatory annotations where necessary but the emphasis is on clear, colourful, sequential illustrations which tell their own story. In order to make their wallcharts more efficacious, some organizations such as Stanley Tools Ltd are also providing them in A3 size with full permission to photocopy in order that pupils can refer to their own copy when the teacher is referring to the full size copy at the front of the class.

Posters

Above all, these can provide colour and interest to the vast vacant wall space of the average comprehensive, thereby making the school more hospitable and perhaps discouraging vandalism. Many subjects dear to the heart of pupils are covered, vehicles of all descriptions, pop stars (publicity material of the recording companies), pets and sport. One category that stands out is that available from tourist offices and airline companies such as Lufthansa and Air India where the posters have true artistic merit.

Maps

These can range in size from hand-sized town plans produced by the Midland Bank and small-scale country maps, depicting economic information available from various countries' embassies (ideal for photocopying), to large-scale pictorial sheets from the same source on specific aspects of the country, as in the case of the Netherlands which has one available on recently reclaimed areas. Other examples include those produced sporadically by the government, such as the Office of Population Census and Survey's *People in Britain* detailing population, density patterns for the whole of the United Kingdom, and organizations like Best Western Hotels chain with an excellent full-size map of Britain showing discreetly where its hotels can be found, but also conveying much useful geographical information, and international airlines' maps depicting the world with major routes and distances.

Postcards

Excellent illustrations on such topics as prehistoric life, birds and animals as well as historic subjects like costume and art itself are to be found as low-cost resources, available generally from the major museums and art galleries. The Post Office also has postcards with pictures of the new stamps as they appear and as these are often based on fundamental aspects of British life—folklore, inventions, famous people etc, they can prove an interesting educational item. Each card can be reinforced with transparent plastic for durability and used as a reference aid, particularly for drawing from when a particular picture is required on one of the subjects covered and so saving the use of books which may be required for more academic study.

Types of materials

Films

Free films of educational value in 16mm format are available on loan on most subjects and are well worth the cost of return postage which has to be paid by the school. Even this cost can be discounted to some extent as sponsors of this medium are also making them available on video cassette where a saving of up to 75% can be made on postage; and the Central Film Library has, from November 1980, provided return carriage via Securicor on two titles or more booked simultaneously.

The potential of film as a teaching resource is reflected in the fact that many are booked up to a year ahead, which unfortunately means a good deal of careful planning if they are to be slotted into a relevant area of the curriculum. Most are sponsored for publicity or promotional purposes, but such is the professionalism in the film making world that it rarely intrudes on the information content of the film. Taking this a stage further, many films made in this country are entered for the various awards of the British Industrial and Sponsored Film Awards (BISFA), which encourages high standards, whilst one need look no further than the many free films of Canada House for an excellence that is founded on the fact that the father of documentary film, John Grierson, originated the Film Board of Canada.

Kits and samples

Raw materials at varying stages of manufacture such as natural and man-made fibres, certain essential cooking ingredients, beverages, paper and different types of woods are available from the industries and any organizations representing them, such as the Timber Research and Development Association, British Wool Marketing Board and the Commonwealth Institute. The samples may have been assembled in the form of an educational kit with accompanying notes as in the case of the British Wool Marketing Board. Sometimes, in this case, a small charge is levied. Sometimes they are provided free without any special packaging or mounted display provision. Either way they can prove an interesting and enlightening resource.

Speakers

City schools and those in areas of high population potentially have access to more individuals prepared to speak to students than their rural counterparts, for even where a speaker is prepared to offer his services free, travel expenses have to be paid. However, the regional counterparts of the nationalized industries are usually able to provide a service entirely free, an example followed often by private firms, especially the financial institutions and individual representatives of the professions, charitable bodies and societies.

Types of materials

The lectures and talks given are often more suitable for the older pupils especially where they are concerned with careers and work experience, an area of increasing potential when local education authorities and industry have devised schemes together. It is essential, therefore, to be acquainted with any local policy that has been formulated in this direction.

REFERENCES

1   Department of Education and Science. *International Understanding: sources of information on international organizations—a handbook for schools and colleges.* DES 1979. 159. Free.
2   Williams, T Michael *Curriculum Decision-making and Educational Television.* Independent Broadcasting Authority 1979. 284. Free.
3   David, John *Energy to Use or Abuse.* Shell UK Ltd 1976. 186. Free.
4   Godson, J and Shapiro, L (ed) *The Soviet Worker: illusions and realities.* Macmillan Press Ltd, 1981. 291. Free.
5   Information Division, Ministry of Culture. *Singapore '82.* High Commission of the Republic of Singapore. London 1982. 270. Free.

3

Sources of materials

Low-cost resources, which can be invaluable in the comprehensive school, originate from a variety of organizations such as central and local government, industry, professional groups, charities, embassies and tourist offices.

These organizations usually have well financed publicity and information departments keen to distribute material for some ulterior motive. This may be for altruistic reasons, say in the case of charities, a combination of public relations and advertising, in the case of private industry, while as far as government funded departments are concerned, the need to keep the public informed has become a matter of policy.

Where an organization has received a demand from schools this has stimulated the formation of education departments specializing in the production of suitable resources. Such departments can usually be relied on to produce quality material which, even if priced, will be heavily subsidised. A free catalogue will often be provided listing what is available.

Central government

The materials issued by government departments are probably the best documented. Information about them can be found in the HMSO *Sectional Lists*, the *Sales List of Reference Documents* and the *Printed Photographic Display Material* of the Central Office of Information, all of which except for the first, for which a small charge is made, are free, and which can be received regularly on a standing order basis.

A good summary of the different kinds of resources available can be seen at a glance in the leaflet by the Central Office of Information— *Services Available to the United Kingdom Public* (COI Reference Division). Perhaps it is not the entirely free publications that are included that could prove the most useful. For an average price of 20p there are many concise documents or factsheets covering most aspects of British life and the Commonwealth.

Details of films, video-cassettes and filmstrips are set out in the *Central Film Library Catalogue* although a *Free Film Supplement* is available. The two other affiliated film libraries in Scotland and Wales also have catalogues which contain free films not found elsewhere. The Scottish Film Library comes under the aegis of the Scottish Council for Technology and whereas its catalogue together with an annual subscription costs rather more than its English counterpart, a good number of the jointly-held films which are available for hire are cheaper, or in fact free. The Welsh Film Library has the smallest collection of films of the three libraries. It is, however, the only source of film on the Principality. Its catalogue is free and will be sent as it is updated if a standing order is placed.

Some government departments produce invaluable free source books, of which three are particularly useful. *The Commonwealth: a guide to material and information services available to schools and to the public*, is produced by the Central Office of Information, the most recent edition being 1977. The second publication is from the Department of Education and Science entitled *International Understanding: sources of information on international organisations*, dated 1979, but nevertheless very useful. The final booklet is *Overseas Development and Aid: a guide to sources of material, 1977*, prepared by the Minister of Overseas Development and the Central Office of Information. It lists 33 organizations from Action in Distress to World Development Movement and through its index links them to over 150 possible topic areas of interest to schools.

Government supported agencies

This group of organizations is at the heart of many important aspects of our society and they are generally regarded as the most authoritative in their field. They produce material for publicity and education purposes independently of official government departments and so a major proportion of their publications including posters do not appear in HMSO *Sectional Lists*. One of their principal aims being to take a lead and to inculcate the highest standards in their area, they are to the fore in providing free material. Catalogues of resources are usually available on request.

While many government supported agencies such as the British Standards Institution, the Metrication Board or the Sports Council (in fact the ones that would receive most of our attention for resource purposes) are well known, there are a considerable number which do not receive so much publicity. Whereas *Whitaker's Almanack* would be the source for the principal agencies, for the others it would be necessary to consult the list called *Quangos: a definitive survey* by Philip Holland MP.

To emphasize the need to consult the agencies' own catalogues of resources, as opposed to relying on the HMSO lists, it is worth taking as an example the Forestry Commission. Its catalogue carries in addition to the priced publications listed by HMSO in *Sectional List No 31*:

a. Any other government literature relating to forestry.

b. A number of non-parliamentary publications no longer stocked by HMSO.

c. Unpriced (free) information pamphlets.

d. Research and development papers.

e. Miscellaneous items (some free, including posters).

It can be seen that some potentially useful material would be omitted if the *Sectional List* alone were relied on.

In cases where a government agency is regionally represented in some form then the nearest office of the organization should be contacted as further resources may be forthcoming. For instance, there may be a national park, a new town, an atomic power station or an arts council in the locality. These would be representative of the Countryside Commission, the New Town Corporation, the Atomic Energy Authority and the Arts Council of Great Britain respectively. It may prove worthwhile later if comprehensive material is required to contact all the regional counterparts of, say, the national parks or atomic energy power stations and build up sufficient resources for class use. For, as has been stated, the agencies are given much independence and are responsible for creating a wealth of first class free or low-cost material.

Local government and public utilities

Local government, together with other important public services like the area health and water authorities can provide sources of primary material useful in many aspects of the school curriculum. The information from councils is *usually* free and obtainable from their publicity or public relations department. It may take the form of an official handbook to a town or region, a year book listing all the council's activities, a budget synopsis, a plan or map, or copious notes on how a council functions. Individual departments within a council should be able to answer specific enquiries on such topics as local industry, consumer affairs and urban growth.

In the case of large public utilities, like a regional water board, in addition to the official statistics, there can be, within these organiz-ations, due to the prevalence of education departments, specially prepared material for schools such as charts, posters or booklets. (The use of telephone directories and the *Municipal Year Book* enable one to trace relevant addresses in this section).

Teachers' professional associations

The Council of Subject Teaching Association lists 30 such bodies as members representing every subject taught throughout the curriculum in secondary schools. Some subjects, such as religious studies, languages and mathematics are represented by more than one Association. In a number of cases the Associations have acquired a prestige and are indisputably the leaders in their field. The Historical Association and the Geographical Association are the two best examples.

The addresses of the Associations can be found listed in the *Education Committee Year Book*, whilst those not members of the above Council, which is not an inconsiderable number, are to be located in *Information Services in Education*, a British Library Research and Development Report No 5448.

Annual subscriptions upward of £10 are payable in some cases, but as well as an enquiry and advisory service, use of the Association's library and reduced rates for low-cost publications and a quality journal may be available to members.

In many respects teachers' professional associations are by their very nature highly specialized and their services more geared to individual teaching staff, but many of them will not be members or perhaps even be aware that an association relevant to them exists. That the associations do inculcate high standards and encourage a deeper awareness of their subject there is no doubt. They provide a stimulus in using new teaching materials and thus shed more light on the creative use of resources. They also provide a current awareness service in their particular subject.

Indirectly they therefore have much to offer in guiding the school librarian towards appropriate resources especially in areas where a specialist knowledge is required. It is to be hoped that heads of individual subject departments will have taken it upon themselves to enrol as members of a representative association and the librarian should be in a position to liaise over the full use of the services offered, perhaps encouraging a greater use of them by being prepared to do the extra administrative work that might be necessary.

Professional and similar groups

Organizations representing the professions and allied trade and product institutes offer much useful information about themselves. They are usually well endowed and respected organizations with departments funded specifically to answer enquiries of an educational nature. Publications, often updated annually, are generally available for the asking and, where appropriate, samples of products may be requested.

The principal area where the above information is useful is that of careers education. Cassells' *Careers Encyclopedia* contains a virtually exhaustive list of relevant addresses, all of which are useful sources of information. It is worth noting, however, that many of the organizations listed distribute annually to all local authority career services their main pamphlets and posters on job opportunities. These are then re-distributed within the authority. It is therefore worth checking locally to see if it is possible to have the school placed on the local distribution list in order to save time and postage.

Organizations representing a product such as the Potato Marketing Board, the British Farm Product Council or White Fish Authority or a service like the British Insurance Association or General Council of British Shipping are listed to a limited extent in *Treasure Chest for Teachers*. Other source books in part given over to listing these organizations and encompassing all those known will be covered in depth later.

Charitable organizations

These organizations can be found listed in the *Charities Digest*, published by the Family Welfare Association. Other useful source books are the *Social Services Year Book* and *Voluntary Social Services Handbook* (National Council of Social Service). Most of the larger charities mount special campaigns from time to time advertised in the national and local press; it is possible then to take advantage of the new publicity and information material available by writing to the sources mentioned in the paper.

The larger charities like Oxfam, Multiple Sclerosis Society, Shelter and the Church of England Children's Society publish their own free newsletters or periodicals. These may well emanate from an education department which, in the case of Shelter, has produced a wide range of low-cost resources designed to increase pupils' awareness about other peoples' problems. The information can provide the backbone for school assembly readings, Civics, individual project work in Religious Education lessons or be used to stimulate a class into selecting a good cause for their annual donation, if such as thing is school policy.

Special interest and pressure groups

Organizations within this grouping have increased dramatically in recent years. Many of them are supported and run by well qualified individuals and, in some cases, have attained a high degree of respectability as in the case of Friends of the Earth and Amnesty International. They have, in the main, well organized education departments producing low-cost quality material.

The area dealing with the preservation and enhancement of the environment is well covered by these groups. Three excellent sources of information exist, with the groups themselves also providing extensive lists of further helpful organizations. The groups are the Conservation Society, the Council for Environmental Education based at Reading University and the Town and Country Planning Association. Each has a small annual subscription but updated reviews of resources appear in their regular bulletins. Individual lists of further sources can be purchased separately like that produced by the Conservation Society which cost 20p in 1978, and which contains details of about 180 organizations together with their addresses.

Overseas development, with an emphasis on Third World countries, is another area covered in detail. The principal sources are the Centre for World Development Education which produces an annual free catalogue of free and low-cost material including further specialized source books on individual countries, and the Council for Education in World Citizenship's *World Studies Resource Guide* with supplements which cost 40p in 1978.

Outside these two broad areas are numerous other groups; virtually every organized activity has a representative body acting as its spokesman. These can be contacted for information about themselves which they are usually only too keen to provide, having in many cases literature prepared especially for such enquiries.

Some groups may be out-and-out pressure groups like the Anti-Fluoridation Campaign and National Anti-Vivisection Society, others less strong in their views like the British Association for the Advancement of Science or the Soil Association, or they may be generally regarded simply as spokesmen for a commendable activity as in the case of the British Canoe Union or the Arab Horse Society.

Two general source books listing these groups are *Directory of Pressure Groups, Representative Associations* and *Directory of British Associations and Associations in Ireland.*

Embassies and tourist offices

The London Diplomatic List provides a record of current addresses whilst *Treasure Chest for Teachers* gives a brief summary of services provided by a select number of these which are known to have educational material.

Not all embassies have associated tourist offices or cultural sections but all generally provide free information pamphlets and possibly an annual handbook of their country containing valuable statistics. Maps and posters, and perhaps a periodical, may also be available, though the latter could bear a small charge, like those offered from the Chinese and South African Embassies. Such journals are usually well produced and contain information not easily found elsewhere (which could be said for the other publications of some legations). Those available gratis are just as valuable and provide a current insight into a nation's affairs as does *Scala* from the West German office.

Films are a rich resource within this category of organization. Whilst they are all generally of high quality, it is not surprising that some have a hire fee. This will be clearly stated in the catalogues available from the embassies. Some countries' films are, however, handled by an agency like Guild Sound and Vision or Viscom, whose catalogues might bear a charge, even if the films themselves are free.

Nationalized industries

These generally cover the basic areas of energy, public transport, communication and iron and steel, a total of 12 major industries, though the government has recently been selling off certain profitable sectors. *Whitaker's Almanack* and *Britain—an official handbook*, provide an up-to-date summary of the situation together with relevant addresses.

The industries vary greatly as sources of information. In general the larger they are the more material is available and this is reflected in the catalogues they issue which are comprehensive and updated annually in the case of the National Coal Board, Electricity Council, British Gas Corporation, British Steel Corporation and the Post Office, but irregular and insubstantial in the case of British Rail and the British Waterways Board, and non-existent in the case of British Aerospace.

In the best instances the resources emanating from an education department will consist of films, filmstrips, posters, publications, wallcharts and speakers, and be in multiple copies of good quality and generally free. The local area boards of the industries should also be able to supplement any material.

Industrial firms

Private industry is able to supply a wealth of resources useful in the comprehensive school. These range from the specially prepared, priced, educational kits and publications of firms like Unilever and BP through to the free films, samples, advertising leaflets and journals of such firms as Woolworth's, David Gelantine, Abu and Ford respectively.

Addresses of firms nationally can be found in publications such as the two *Kelly's Directories* and the telephone directories. Specific information on services they might offer and the likelihood of resources being available can be sought in the annual *Register of Members of the*

Institute of Public Relations, which lists the departments usually associated with the provision of material, and *Treasure Chest for Teachers*.

The Understanding British Industry (UBI) project should be publishing a comprehensive resource directory of firms producing educational type resources. Currently they have available only a short list of relevant firms which is useful and free. Many more likely firms can be found as they advertise in the national and local press, including specialist magazines.

Some caution should be exercised as some firms in their advertising, especially those representing popular interests like motoring, shooting and fishing, request a charge to cover postage, handling and even the cost of catalogues or leaflets advertising the goods. Such firms are to be avoided as experience has proved that similar if not better material can be obtained free from rival companies.

Large firms with education departments produce comprehensive catalogues of resources which, if bearing a charge, will be clearly marked as such. The catalogue from ICI's Schools' Liaison Section is an excellent example, listing resources obtainable from Head Office (with an order form), then giving addresses of its various divisions together with their available publications and finally a list of useful addresses of educational organizations and other companies providing resources.

Currency of low-cost resources

To conclude this chapter it is of value to cover briefly the essentials of keeping up-to-date with material that has been found to be of use.

Some organizations have a regular newsletter or bulletin listing new and existing material. In the case, therefore, of Shell, the Schools Information Centre on the Chemical Industry, the Council of Europe or the Commission for Racial Equality, it is essential to be placed on their mailing list. Similar to this is being on the mailing list of those organizations which make a point of sending new material, if and when it appears, to those interested in receiving it. Oxfam, the Bank Education Service and the Welsh Office are examples here.

Other new material might be reviewed or even advertised in the educational press. *The Times Educational Supplement* heads the list for such information followed by the *Teacher, Education Guardian* and *The Financial Times*, with its regular video and film article on the technology page on Tuesdays.

Reports and findings on current problems are covered in the quality papers like *The Times, The Guardian* and *The Daily Telegraph*; the last is the best for stating the bibliographical details of any publication mentioned. The papers as well as BBC national radio, with its well-researched documentaries identifying information areas perhaps better than television, are also important in keeping abreast of possible and potential sources. Above all it is essential for the librarian to be well informed of current trends in society.

On a provincial basis the local media will reveal personalities and organizations of potential use. The activities of Rotary Clubs, Round Tables, Women's Institutes and similar groups reveal speakers who might offer their services to schools, whilst special supplements in the press on local industry identify firms with active public relations departments.

It will be necessary to send off annually for some materials, like embassy year books or film catalogues of known agencies. In some cases it will be worthwhile to renew materials, like posters and leaflets, on a regular basis, perhaps every six months, and this would automatically reveal anything new, although it is possible that some organizations, such as the Dairy Council, who operate a quota system, keep a record of what is sent to a school and limit the supply.

4

Subject areas

In any secondary school the librarian must think in terms of the curriculum and, therefore, this survey of materials is divided up according to the subject areas most commonly used in schools.

Inevitably there is some overlap in materials which could be appropriate in more than one area, especially in such subjects as geography, environmental studies and general studies. Where this is the case, due recognition is given, and the reader made aware of further references.

Whilst subjects are arranged alphabetically, the material within them does not lend itself to such a formal pattern. In each case resources are dealt with in the way most appropriate and logical for that subject—depending on the number of existing source books, the variety of sources and the different types of material encountered.

It is assumed that the librarian liaises closely with the various subject departments and is fully aware of the developments in the curriculum. Matching new resources to what is required ensures a healthy and efficient service, encouraging more use to be made of it. Cooperation and mutual help are thus engendered which is especially relevant where certain departments pursue restrictive practices regarding the use of material.

Art

In the field of art, the main need of teachers is for specialist material, and this depends to a large extent on the amount of advanced level work taught in the school and the department's holdings in basic texts, central to the teaching and learning element of the subject. It is true to say in an essentially practical subject like art, little of the department's allowance can be made available for academic resources for a minority whose number can also fluctuate widely from year to year. It might well be that only through the public library service will students have access to basic texts, whilst in extreme cases, where very specialist subjects are pursued for projects, individuals will have to purchase their own books. However, a number of relevant outside organizations will be able to help and a thorough grounding in these and the forging of strong links with them will enable pupils in most cases to have access to all the information they require.

Before discussing the provision for information, a note on art competitions could prove useful as they can stimulate creativity and provide an objective for the pupils. Details of some can be found in *Arts Review*, but there is no current definitive list. Some may be on a local basis organized for instance through local radio or the County Naturalist Trust. Charities often run a poster competition which would be publicized in their newsletters, as do nationalized industries such as the Post Office, when schools could be notified individually of the rules. Children's television programmes, the national newspapers and large firms also have competitions from time to time. In general, the librarian must be vigilant and, when a competition is identified, send for details in order to publicize them within the school. One national art competition which involved designing a poster was, according to its originators, the Commission for Racial Equality, the largest of its kind ever held in Britain, with over 40,000 schools involved. Three major unions, a national newspaper and a bank were just some of its sponsors putting forward a total of £5,000 in prizes. The success of this could well mean more use of art competitions for publicity purposes.

To the art teacher, the librarian's information file will provide details of groups based at the teachers' centre, the facilities offered by museums, art galleries/centres and relevant public library services such as a picture loan collection and the collections of the local art college, with any conditions of loan agreements. Once aware of these specialized resources, staff would be in a position to build up their own contacts in areas of particular interest to themselves.

The librarian must make available information about current activity in the local art world. All the Regional Art Associations publish free bulletins which list 'What's on and where?' in the area. As many of the activities, exhibitions and talks are heavily subsidized or free, they can provide worthwhile events for school outings. The bulletins may also contain useful articles on various aspects of art which are worth filing for reference. Two low-cost publications of the Arts Council itself—*Arts Council Bulletin*, a monthly information document containing news of its development, and *Arts in Action*, are both of value in the library.

The *Arts Review*, although not itself a low-cost item, is invaluable amongst the commercially produced journals for keeping abreast of the art scene, both at home and abroad and for reviewing or advertising possible sources of materials; it does identify new and existing low-cost material.

The Arts Council publishes a wide range of useful booklets of which the *Catalogues of Art Exhibitions* are excellent value. These are well illustrated and, costing from fifteen to fifty pence, cover a wide range of subjects from the organization's own collection to specialist areas like Oriental art, architecture and individual artists.

The Arts Council, many musuems and art galleries produce low-cost postcards on a wide variety of artistic subjects, which reflect the specialist interest of the originating institution. Thus the National Gallery is excellent for Old Masters, the Victoria and Albert Museum for costume and the Birmingham Museum and Art Gallery for drawings by the Pre-Raphaelites.

The Society for Education through Art has some usefully succinct low priced publications covering such areas as children and creative painting, screen printing, dyes and dyeing and clay modelling.

Certain organizations are able to offer free advice and guidance for the study of architecture. First on the list must come the Royal Institute of British Architects who can recommend a member in the area to talk on any particular aspect required. The same service is provided by the Civic Trust, a highly active group devoted to protecting and improving the environment, particularly in relation to old buildings, a favourite topic for such talks. Other similar organizations are the Society for the Protection of Ancient Buildings and the Historic Buildings Council, which gives grants to preserve places of national importance, again places which might be in the area and suitable for study. The planning department of the local authority can also be contacted for information on its listed properties.

Newspapers: colour supplements

The Sunday colour supplements are undoubtedly an important area of free material in the arts. The articles are well written, erudite, usually of a topical interest and very well illustrated. The following examples, chosen at random, indicate the coverage and emphasize the need to collect and organize these articles into a useful reference file.

General interest

'Painters who have changed the course of history' (*The Observer* 15/9/74).
'Royal Academy Summer Exhibition' (*Sunday Telegraph* 30/5/75).

Subject areas

'Art Galleries' *(Sunday Telegraph* 30/1/76).
'Art of India' *(The Observer* 1/8/82).
'Fashion museum' *(Sunday Times* 6/8/82).
'Vatican Spectacular' *(Sunday Telegraph* 1/5/83).
'Taking Art off the Streets' *(Sunday Times* 14/8/83).
'Caricatures' *(The Observer* 4/9/83).
'The Greatest Story ever Painted' *(Sunday Times* 4/12/83).

Architecture

'Language of architecture' *(Sunday Times* 18/8/75).
'National Trust houses' *(Sunday Telegraph* 22/8/75).
'The Spire of Salisbury' *(Sunday Telegraph* 14/11/75).
'The architect of an English Eden: Sir Geoffrey Jellicoe' *(Sunday Times* 15/8/82).
'Charles Rennie Mackintosh' *(The Observer* 21/8/83).
'Modern Monuments: Nuremburg' *(The Observer* 2/10/83).
'A Place in the Country: the cult of the cottage' *(Sunday Times* 3/10/82).
'Ernest George Trobridge: Castles in Suburbia' *(The Observer* 14/11/82).

Artists

'Durer' *(Sunday Telegraph* 21/5/71).
'Turner' *(Sunday Times* 10/11/74).
'Hockney' *(The Observer* 2/2/75).
'Constable' *(The Observer* 15/2/76).
'Leonid Pasternak' *(Sunday Times* 12/6/83).
'Monet' *(Sunday Times* 1/5/83).
'Anthony Green' *(The Observer* 22/5/83).
'Various contemporary artists' *(Sunday Times* 22/5/83).
'Duffy Sheridan' *(Sunday Times* 12/6/83).
'Michael Leonard' *(Sunday Times* 2/10/83).

Art Movements

'Constructurists Group' *(The Observer* 26/1/69).
'Early Impressionists' *(Sunday Telegraph* 8/2/74).
'Surrealism: Giorgio de Chirico' *(Sunday Times* 1/8/82).
'Cubism' *(Sunday Times* 24/4/83).
'Edouard Manet' *(Sunday· Times* 5/6/83).
'Russian Satirical journals' *(Sunday Times* 4/9/83).

Individual Paintings

'Card Players' (*The Observer* 17/6/79) (One of a series).

Photography

'H Talbot—Father of Photography' (*Sunday Times* 6/7/75).
'Birth of colour photography' (*Sunday Times* 8/3/75).
'Nostalgic photography' (*Sunday Times* 28/7/76).
'Photo finish' (*Sunday Times* 6/8/82).
'Nature Photography' (*Sunday Times* 24/10/82).
'Emile Zola: Photographer' (*The Observer* 27/2/83).
'Vanity Fair' (*Sunday Times* 20/3/83).
'Snap Judgements' (*Sunday Times* 3/4/83).
'Night Trains: Winston Link' (*Sunday Times* 19/6/83).
'Portraits with a Touch of Karsh' (*Sunday Times* 3/7/83).
'Portraits from a Glossy Life: Norman Parkinson' (*Sunday Times* 31/7/83).
'Studies in Truth: Snowdon' (*Sunday Times* 25/9/83).
'Photographs that turn into Fine Art' (*Sunday Times* 24/10/83).

Newspapers

These can also yield articles of substance in obituaries and on such topics as exhibitions and trends in the arts. This information, if filed away, can also have a possible use in the general studies field. Such a person as L S Lowry created this dual interest, and newspaper articles must have been a primary source of information on his life and work with books being both very expensive and scarce at the time of his death.

Films

This material is available on virtually all aspects of art for a hire charge in many cases of less than £2, and in some cases, without any charge. There will, of course, be the cost of return postage.

The Scottish Film Library (SFL) offers the largest selection of low-cost films, though with impending price increases this could be reduced. In its classified catalogue are over 170 potentially useful titles, well distributed across the principal areas of the subject.

The scope of this source is highlighted with the following examples: (as there is no key to the abbreviations used for the film producers in the catalogue, only those which the author could deduce are written in full).

Philosophy and Theory

Art and Movement (Education Films of Scotland) Colour 18 minutes.
Discovering Harmony in Art (BHF) Colour 16 minutes.
Is Art Necessary? (Associated Television) Black/white 26 minutes.

Sculpture

Barbara Hepworth at the Tate (British Film Institute) Black/white 12 minutes.
Clay in Action (Great Britain) Black/white 11 minutes.
Epstein (BBC/TV) Black/white 14 minutes.

Drawing

Vertical (British Film Institute) Colour 18 minutes.
Drawing a Portrait (EB) Colour 4 minutes.

Painting

Albrecht Durer (BBC/TV) Black/white 9 minutes.
Dutch Masterpieces (Netherlands Gallery) Black/white 17 minutes.
(A further 25 major painters are covered).

Photography

Magic of Photography (RH) Black/white 10 minutes.
Facts About Film (BHF) Colour 17 minutes.

The Educational Foundation for Visual Aids (EFVA) has fewer titles listed in its catalogues, but is nevertheless very comprehensive. Its films tend to be more expensive which may reflect on their quality, a significant number being produced by Encyclopedia Britannica and the Educational Foundation for Visual Aids itself, where the hire fee is in excess of £5. Of note, however, are the films produced by the Netherlands and Belgian governments (the Educational Foundation for Visual Aids acting as distributor). In these two cases, hire charges are well within our low-cost definition and may illustrate the point of hidden subsidy in material sponsored by an institution. There are, for instance, two films listed called *Rembrandt*, one produced by Encyclopedia Britannica, the other by the Dutch Government, each in essence covering the painter's life and work. The first has a hire charge of £10, the second £1.

The Central Film Library has only a dozen general films on art. Three titles of note, *Picture Post*, *After the Arrow* and *The Rainbow Verdict*, produced by the Post Office, were transferred to the latter's own agency in late 1979. They are all free and make excellent viewing for art purposes, although the subject is stamps.

George Rowney and Company Ltd, manufacturers of artists materials since 1789, have two free films available. The titles are *Pigments to Palette* on artists colours and *Cryla* (acrylic colour), each approximately 18 minutes long.

The remaining films available for hire at a low-cost are all produced by certain individual governments, and are usually available from the embassies concerned. In the case of some Eastern European countries, Educational and Television Films Ltd (ETV) act as distributor. The films generally concentrate on important artists and art galleries, and on the historical aspect of art and culture within the country.

Educational and Television Films Ltd, representing the countries of Czechoslovakia, USSR, Bulgaria and the German Democratic Republic, has a wide selection of films on offer. In general, costs preclude them from inclusion here. However the topics covered such as puppetry and cartoons could make them of interest, costs not withstanding. On the other hand, the West German Film Library has more of significance to offer with a notable collection of over 30 films, all free and well produced. The artists represented are Beckmann, Bosch, Cranach, Durer, Friedrich, Holbein, Kandinsky, Klee and Kobell.

Other European countries with low-cost films which could prove useful in the art room are Finland (architecture and sculpture), Hungary and Poland (costume and posters). Other countries are represented to a large extent by films reflecting primitive art such as Australia with the Aborigine, South Africa and the Bushmen, Canada and the Red Indian, and India.

Illustrations

Finally, one of the most demanding areas where the library is called upon to help in the subject of art is that of providing illustrations for individual pupils to work from. It is here that the wealth of free leaflets, brochures and posters can be of enormous help in relieving the demand for books. Fortunately too, some of the best examples of free material available from firms coincide with the popular areas chosen by the children—aircraft, farm machinery, horses, lorries, motor cars, pets, ships and weapons. For other popular subjects such as birds, flowers and costume, the postcards from the various museums are an excellent proposition. Files of illustrations can be built up, cutting up old magazines and books for the purpose. Some pictures may be worth preserving, as indeed the postcards are, with a protective film to prolong usage.

Sources of illustrative material on most of the popular topics are readily available from advertisements in the magazines read by the pupils. These include such titles as *Motor, Commercial Motor, Motor Cycle News, Power Farming, Shooting Times, Airgun World* and *Pony*. For products not made in this country then the concessionaires must be contacted for the best brochures and leaflets—this is especially applicable in the case of cars and motorcycles. A knowledge of firms' products is, of course, essential in tracking down likely sources of material. *Kelly's Directories* are invaluable here as are company annual reports appearing in the business pages of the quality newspapers, where companies' activities are itemized. The 'Observers' series of books published by Warne covering popular topics can also prove invaluable, as addresses of principal manufacturers are given—though this information has been lacking in recent editions. Interesting and useful examples here included tanks and armoured fighting vehicles with Alvis as an excellent source for lavishly produced coloured booklets, British Aerospace (Warton division) with superb posters on the Tornado jet and Westland Helicopters of Yeovil for colour posters on a wide range of helicopters.

There is some excellent illustrative material of interest to girls from the large chain stores specializing in fashionable clothes. Two examples are British Home Stores with 'press release' packages composed of large black and white photographs depicting models in their new lines, and colourful posters from Miss Selfridge. This material is, of course, updated regularly, at least twice a year for the winter and summer ranges.

Another popular topic for drawing is animals, especially horses, with *Pony* magazine providing a number of sources from which coloured illustrations can be obtained. Pharmaceutical and animal feed firms appear throughout the magazine, though a glimpse in a veterinary surgeon's waiting room will quickly reveal the best examples of posters on the subject. An excellent example here is Duphar of Southampton. Pedigree Petfoods make available for schools a 'jackdaw' folder on pets, perhaps one of the best examples of a free educational resource there is. This comprises a teacher's handbook, two wallcharts, six illustrated work cards and seven practical classroom activity sheets on dogs and cats.

Single photocopies of popular subjects can also be used to supplement books, the lack of colour being compensated to some extent by the basic requirements for an outline to copy from. Science fiction and 'horror' topics are likely areas for consideration—where the black and white picture can serve to stimulate a pupil's imagination.

In conclusion, it is worth encouraging the art department to build up its own collection of the above materials, under the library's guidance, in order to have a range of ready-reference material readily to hand during the course of lessons.

Business Studies, Commerce, Economics and Money Management

All these subjects have common elements in their respective syllabuses for which there is a useful amount of relevant material; all to some extent concern themselves with trade, the business units of industry, the economy, taxation and especially the commercial services of the major financial institutions. The major financial institutions all produce educational resources and as they are so invaluable and distinctly unique it is worth examining them in detail.

Building societies

The Building Societies Association is responsible for a wide variety of low-cost material and this is outlined in its brochure entitled *Teaching Aids*. The range available, most of which can be obtained in multiple copies, includes booklets, wallcharts, a study pack, journals and speakers. It is possible to be placed on a mailing list in order to receive new material as and when it is published. For the lower ability child there are two illustrated booklets—*10,000 Years of Money* and *2,000 Years of Houses*. The first tells in a readable style the history of money, its importance in daily life as well as outlining various forms of investment in banks, the stock exchange, national savings and building societies.

The second publication describes the development of housing from the primitive farmstead of 20 BC to the housing of the 1970s. Each major stage is illustrated and the important social and economic factors influencing the changes in housing are described. Both these publications provide a basic introduction to the importance of the Building Society Movement and what it has to offer for 10 to 16 year-olds.

Of value to older pupils are *One Day*—a project booklet for senior students and *The Role of the Building Societies*. Each describes in some depth various aspects of housing and the management of building societies and their deposits.

The other booklets available are of interest to staff and perhaps the sixth former. The most substantial is *Building Societies and House Purchase*, a comprehensive guide to investment, house purchase, insurance and the home saver. The booklet concludes with sources of additional information listing the names and addresses of those organizations who are worth contacting, such as the Department of the Environment and the National House Building Council. The other three publications, *Savings Facts*, *Housing Facts* and *Facts About Building Societies* contain principally current statistics and other data.

The study pack, *Building Societies: study folder*, contains all the booklets mentioned previously as well as additional material. Teachers' notes give guidance on the use of it and provide suggestions for further work. The value of the folder is enhanced with the provision of six work cards, each card suggesting an area of study based on the material with the complete set providing a wide coverage of the subject, both on the practical side of house purchase and on the broad context of housing past and present. Supplementary to the work card programme are 12 study prints, each covering further aspects of choosing, buying and running a home, and the work of the building societies.

Akin to the *Study Folder*, but at a far more advanced level (perhaps because the material has been produced in conjunction with the Economics Association), is the *'A' Level Economics Study Kit*, comprised of eight topic papers illustrating the application of basic economic concepts—demand, supply, price determination, interest rate determination, industrial organization and economics of scale, savings and consumption. Needless to say all examples relate to the building society field. The topic papers are supplemented with a source book of data relating to the United Kingdom economy and the United Kingdom housing market. Such data include national income and expenditure, prices, sources and distribution of income.

The journals available include *Building Society News*, a four-page digest of current news affecting the societies, with statistical data on their assets, liabilities and advances and the more heavyweight *BSA Bulletin* which covers the same area but in far greater depth. The statistical information is well presented in a variety of methods from straight tabulations to maps, graphs and charts.

Two films can be obtained, both are well produced, being both entertaining and instructive. *The Strongest Link* deals with an average working day experienced in a building society emphasizing its importance in the financial life of the community, whilst *Sam's Song* illustrates the two principal functions of borrowing and lending carried out by societies from the personal viewpoint of a young couple wishing to buy a home.

Most local building society managers are only too happy to address groups of pupils whilst, if any difficulties are encountered, the Building Societies Association will help.

One useful publication of relevance here not published by the societies is *Buying a House on an Option Mortgage* from the Department of the Environment.

Bank Education Service (BES)

An excellent range of material is distributed by the service, made especially useful by the fact that it is available in class sets. Fifteen booklets, each covering a specific part of banking such as borrowing, the clearing system or cheques, can be obtained. Added to these are five wallcharts and many examples of actual stationery used in the banking world: forms, cheques, credit slips, giro credits and bank statements. For teaching purposes this material can be grouped under four headings:

Subject areas

a. Usage, the forms of, and supply of money.
b. Transfer of paper money.
c. Creating and borrowing of money.
d. International money.

Of particular note is that the material is constantly being updated, especially any concerned with computers, and practising educationalists help in its preparation. This has resulted in its being constantly reappraised for teaching purposes; as an example, one of the wallcharts, *How to Use a Cheque*, has been redesigned and this, together with the other charts, is also made available in A4 size suitable for photocopying by the teacher in order that pupils can refer to their own copies.

While no films are available from the Bank Education Service, there is a speaker service, with the lecture being tailor-made for the particular occasion in order that it is seen as relevant to the syllabus at that particular time. All topics, catered for at all ability levels, can be dealt with in one or more lectures. Full use of audio-visual aids is made and all in all the talks are both entertaining and meaningful.

Supplementing the excellent resources of the Bank Education Service are, of course, the commercial banks themselves, who must rank as one of the richest sources of free material on the economics field with information ranging from that of general interest such as the Trustee Savings Bank's *Family* magazine covering basic money matters, to the erudite booklet—the *British Banking System*—from the National Westminster Bank.

All banks produce useful leaflets on their services which can be retained for comparative purposes and also used for explaining aspects of banking terminology.

Lloyds Bank have perhaps the widest range of material. Starting with the 90-page book, *What Goes on in the City*, this provides a detailed study of all the major financial institutions and includes a glossary, a bibliography and further sources of information which may be contacted. The *Black Horse Guides* — *When You Start Earning, Tax and Financial Planning, Household and Family Money Management* and *Questions Women Ask About Money* all provide concise accounts on their respective subjects in question and answer format. Two annual publications published by the bank, both of which provide a wealth of statistical data on the country, are the *British Economy in Figures* and an *Economic Profile of Britain*; the latter covers a range of information from population and income through employment, industry and energy to overseas trade and government finance.

The *Reviews* of the banks also provide account statistics and in-depth articles on economic subjects of topical concern. Filed away they can provide a wealth of financial data.

Subject areas

The National Savings Committee

The National Savings Committee, like the Bank Education Service, issues excellent free material on essential money management skills. Booklets include the *Mathematics of Money* with the back-up folder *Making Money Sense—a question of choice* (SL543) which gives sources of information in great detail; *Making Sense in Society* and *Thinking About Money*. Taking a closer look at the first publication one finds in its 60 pages a readable account, supplemented with examples to illustrate terms used, together with a useful array of questions for pupils to complete. Topics covered include aspects of wages, banks, hire purchase, house purchase, finance of contracts, the mathematics of money in commerce, consumer protection, costing and investing. In fact the book would constitute an admirable course on money management for fifth formers.

The British Insurance Association (BIA)

The leaflet *Teaching Aids* outlines all that is available and includes folders (booklets and leaflets in multiple copies), films and speakers with all except the first category being gratis, but even these are free as single specimen items.

The two booklets provide a simple and highly readable introduction to the business of insurance. Each is well illustrated. The leaflets, on the other hand, cover in some detail aspects of different kinds of insurance— buildings, home contents, motor and holiday policies and include information on the discouragement of theft.

For an even more detailed look at the insurance world, then the three study folders must be referred to. Each contains nine study prints, three work cards and teachers' notes on how to get the most out of the material. The titles of these three study folders are self-explanatory—*The History of British Insurance; Insurance for You* and *How an Insurance Company Works*. Each of the study prints is relevant to the subject area with such topics as commerce and insurance, saving and investment, proposal forms and claims assessment. The work cards bring together nicely the topics covered and so provide a comprehensive schedule for testing the pupil's knowledge acquired in the subject.

Three films are obtainable from the Insurance Film Library—*The Square Deal* shows how Britain is the leader in the world insurance league, while *The Risk Takers* and the *Margin of Averages* are mainly concerned with the different jobs involved in insurance, and aimed more at careers education but they are still of general interest as they make for a better understanding of what is by no means an easy world to understand.

Speakers can be arranged to visit the school and lecture on specific topics in a similar manner as that arranged by the Bank Education Service.

Life Offices' Association

The Life Offices' Association acts as spokesman for the major life assurance companies and consequently has much to offer on this important aspect of our economic life.

Starting with examples of the priced material is *Money and You*, aimed at 'O' level students in the commercial and economics field. This is concerned with individual's handling of money under the six main headings of the wage packet, budgeting, getting married, the family budget, saving and borrowing, whilst information sheets on this kit cover national insurance, sales and promotion and the consumer, choosing a home, family protection and saving and credit. Teachers' notes are supplied and contain answers to the set questions as well as suggestions for further projects and topics for discussion. What makes these good value is the fact that the kit provides enough material for six students to use it simultaneously. Another publication is *How Life Insurance Works*—this incorporates cartoons, work cards and examples of stationery, the emphasis on colourful and stimulating presentation.

The free material includes two booklets, wallcharts, a stencil master and a journal. *What is Life Assurance* provides a 16-page, simply worded, well illustrated introduction to the subject whilst *Savings Wise* an an excellent survey of the services of primary financial institutions from the point of view of the investor. Both these publications are available in multiple copies. The wallcharts are a colourful presentation of the terms used in life assurance describing how it works, how policies are taken out, the various forms of policy and words used in drawing up a contract. The stencil master supplements them enabling multiple copies to be made by the school, the most important of which is the specimen proposal form for a life policy. Finally the journal *Money Management Review* contains issues such as government spending, inflation, news and events in the money management field and topics on finance relating to the family budget.

The Stock Exchange Financial Information Service (SEFIS)

A number of free brochures can be obtained outlining the role of this institution—*Why Have a Stock Exchange?*, *How Does the Stock Exchange Work?* and a *Glossary of Terms*. Each deals with its subject in a succinct and readable manner in a question and answer format, and where diagrams or examples make for an easier understanding of the system, then use is made of them. In order to keep up to date with statistical data the quarterly *Stock Exchange Fact Book* can be purchased as a low-cost item on an annual subscription basis. Two wallcharts are available for a small charge, illustrating how a company is formed and financed, and the role of the stock exchange. Finally a free film called *My Word is My Bond* can be borrowed; this shows the importance of the stock exchange as a national institution and how its activities affect two out of three people in Britain.

The Board of Inland Revenue

An important aspect within this subject field is in the area of 'Pay as you earn' taxation. A wide variety of leaflets, forms and pamphlets can be obtained which enable the teacher both to understand the system and to impart the information to pupils with the added benefit of being able to offer the class forms to fill in themselves.

Tutors' notes on PAYE are available providing the basis for lessons applicable to future single wage-earning employees. The leaflets *Paying Tax for the First Time* and *Income Tax and the School Learner* provide a summary of what is required and this can be supplemented with the other leaflets in the series dealing with particular aspects of personal direct taxation—allowances, wife's earnings, the new unified tax system and income tax and the elderly. In addition for staff persual, there are the *Deductions Working Sheet P11, P45 Transfer Document, the Employers Guide to Pay as You Earn,* the forms *P1 Tax Returns* and *P15 Coding Claim.* All the other material can be acquired in class sets on such topics as allowances, codings and deductions. Finally there is the most recent resource from the Inland Revenue Education Service, a *Time Chart* costing £1.25: a journey through time covering the various aspects of taxation, the tax system and its history to the present day.

British Overseas Trade Board (BOTB)

This board of the Department of Trade is able to provide some invaluable material on British exports. *Talking Points on Britain's Economy* is a free monthly pamphlet drawing together Britain's economic achievements on the export front, whilst in-depth surveys of foreign economies and trade are contained in the low-cost 'Occasional paper' series. Examples include *Enlargement of the European Community—Greece, Spain and Portugal* (April 1980), the *UK's Earnings from Invisible Exports* (January 1980) and *Anglo-Japanese Trade* (September 1979). The quarterly *World Economic Comment* and monthly *Review of External Trade Statistics* cannot be classified as low-cost if subscribed to on an annual basis, but individual copies of these can, and, considering the wealth of information they contain, occasional copies can prove indispensible in the library. A knowledge of the British

Overseas Trade Board itself is essential for most finance-based courses and this is covered in depth in the free 42-page booklet on its services.

Department of Industry

Vital information for the more academic source on the way businesses are encouraged, and the way they are financed, is well documented in a series of 20 free booklets published by the Small Firms Information Service, which range from *Starting a Business through Marketing, Raising Finance* and *Moving Location* to *Employing Staff* and *How to Start Exporting.* The information is well presented and all the more interesting from the student's point of view as it is seen in a realistic context. Similar material is available from other offices of the department—the Development Commission, the Council for Small Industries in Rural Areas (COSIRA), the Highlands and Islands Development Board and its Welsh counterpart, as well as local government industrial development offices or planning departments. Such material can be invaluable for pupils undertaking their own individual economic-based projects.

Local authorities

Most local authorities will provide free handbooks and the like, enabling students to ascertain how they are financed and how the money is spent. Take as an example the Greater London Council and the London Boroughs Association. For each there is a general handbook—*London: facts and figures* and the *London Boroughs Association Handbook*, each outlining, through a range of well presented facts and figures, the role and responsibilities each plays, with details of population, services, economic activity and finance. This information can be amplified through consulting further publications such as *The Way the GLC Works*, the *Government of London* and *Annual Budget Diagnosis of the GLC.* Each provides a succinct, readable and comprehensible guide to the topics in question. If even more detailed material is required in the area of finance then the annual financial review and capital revenue estimates can be consulted.

Before leaving the major financial institutions and organizations, mention must be made of those which, while not the most important in terms of producers of material, do, nevertheless, have something of worth to offer. Self-explanatory booklets are available from the following dealing with current facts on the organization's functions and its financial history: the Association of Investment Trust Companies, the Baltic Exchange, the British Insurers Brokers Association, the Committee on Invisible Exports, the Equipment Leasing Association, the Federation of Commodity Associations, the Issuing Houses Association,

London Commodity Exchange, London Discount Market Association, London Metal Exchange, National Association of Pension Funds, Panel on Takeovers and Mergers, the Finance Houses Association and the Unit Trust Association.

Commercial organizations

Information on firms can be gleaned from company annual reports, which contain a mine of information useful to the commercial student. Apart from the presentation of the accounts, other aspects covered include the role of the management team, the functions of subsidiary companies, an explanation of the accounting procedures, profit and loss accounts, capital programming, trading operations, territorial analysis, financial calendars, balance sheets, sources and applications for funds and audited statements. With all these terms being the necessary vocabulary of commerce, seeing them in the context of a firm's trading position makes them all the more valid and real in the student's eyes. Often the annual reports are vividly illustrated and further enhanced for teaching purposes with the inclusion of statistical data displayed in a variety of ways. Needless to say, it is to the giants of the commercial world like ICI and ITT that one should turn for good examples of this form of publication. Supplementing this kind of information are the seven topic papers of Unilever, each outlining important aspects of commercial enterprise:

a. *The Natural History of the Company Director.*
b. *The Multinational in Perspective.*
c. *Managers, Money and Motivation.*
d. *Social Responsibility, the Heart of a Business.*
e. *Food in the Future.*
f. *Decisions Don't Grow on Trees.*
g. *Public Opinion and the Social Market.*

Each is written by a senior manager of the company who has many years experience to call upon.

The Economic Association is the teachers' body which is able to offer relevant material in this section. A wide range of school briefs and work books, occasional papers, case studies, and teachers' handbooks can be obtained. Whilst most are free the majority are low-cost and are good value for money. The fact that many of the items are selected articles from *The Economist* gives them a blueprint of authority and in terms of cost they are far cheaper than the school photocopying them, let alone buying the journal in the first place.

The Aims of Industry, and Facts About Business, both employers organizations, produce some basic booklets of interest for the less academic student. The first publishes *C is for Company*, whilst the second is responsible for *Why Profits* and *Why Investment*.

Complementing these, being produced by the Trades Union Congress, are an *ABC of the TUC, The Union at Work* and *Going to Work.* Others are available at low–cost and include an *Annual Review, Income and Wealth, Industrial Democracy* and *The Social Contract.* These would be sufficient to describe the role, composition, policies, membership figures (taken from the *Employment Gazette*) and terminology of the unions.

The role of advertising in the economic field is well catered for by the Institute of Practitioners in Advertising (IPA). *What Advertising Does* provides a basic reader on the subject, describing its functions and placing it in context within the economic framework of production. Apart from this, the other publications of the Institute of Practitioners in Advertising bear a small charge and cover such topics as marketing, research, trade relations, standards, public relations and the advertising agencies themselves. Titles include *Fifty Years of Advertising, Advertising and the Public* and *The Influence and Techniques of Modern Advertising.*

In conclusion, it is appropriate to mention a series of films produced under the aegis of a group of major companies such as Esso and ICI on the subject of business, economic theory and the world of commerce. The series is called the *Foundations of Wealth* and consists of five 10-minute films, each illustrating the points in question with cartoons and documentary film. The basics of economic growth are well conveyed in an entertaining yet instructive manner and are especially useful for the less academic pupil who could find this subject more than a little daunting.

Careers

Information about work and the working world is invaluable in the school, regardless of whether any active education programme in careers is incorporated within the curriculum. Pupils need to be made aware of what opportunities there are beyond the school gates and indeed will have a natural curiosity to be satisfied. Careers books tend to be expensive and are soon out of date, and their very format can be daunting for most students who are simply looking for basic information. (It must be said, however, that there is no substitute for a good annual edition of a careers encyclopaedia such as Cassell's *Careers Encyclopaedia*.) Fortunately there is a wealth of low-cost material, much of it free, in the form of leaflets and pamphlets, which are a far more attractive proposition to the enquirer. Produced by professional and trade associations, education institutions and training boards, it is accurate and kept up-to-date on matters such as entrance qualifications, opportunities and salaries, making it invaluable in the school.

The degree to which the library may be involved in careers literature will, to a large extent, depend on the school's policy in such matters; for instance, a careers room, together with a member of staff with specific responsibility for careers, and a corresponding reduction in teaching time, may be provided; policy may also be affected by the physical layout of the school—a split site, a sixth form block and the like. Even where careers rooms are provided, it is true to say that few teachers responsible for them admit that enough time is set aside for stocking and organizing the material in them and even fewer can say that pupils have free access to them at all times.

The library can therefore help by acquiring careers information both for itself and for any specialist collection, by offering its organizing expertise, and by generally co-operating to the utmost in maximizing the use of all resources.

Two principal areas of resource provision can be defined: the first is information on jobs generally applicable to pupils up to fifth form level with more specific material for the sixth form, and the second is that of information on further education. In practice the two are interdependent, especially when the school provides an adequate counselling service.

It is worth mentioning the work and facilities of the local authority Careers Service. Their comprehensive service and resources should be well advertised in the school, and a visit by the librarian to see at first hand their library as a possible model, with the range of material available, would be time well spent. One important consideration is to ascertain if, apart from comprehensive information on careers, provision is made for the loan of resources involved in careers education, which may be useful for teachers contemplating such a programme. These resources could range from professional textbooks to surveys, and include simulations, games, teachers' aids and careers programmes with all the necessary equipment for possible lessons throughout any one year.

The Careers and Occupational Information Centre (COIC)

Undoubtedly the Careers and Occupational Information Centre (Manpower Services Commission) is the most important organization in the careers field useful to the school librarian; as the Centre distributes a wealth of free literature it is necessary to be placed on its mailing list. A checklist of items appears in *Newscheck*, its free monthly magazine. This journal is also useful for current information on occupations and industry, and developments in education and training. The types of information the Centre makes available include:

Signposts. A highly stimulating aid for pupils of all abilities, consisting of a card index listing hundreds of jobs which are filed within 10 interest areas enabling the user to be guided from his primary interest to related occupations and thence to the appropriate section of the careers library.

The Careers Library Classification Index (CLCI)

This classification scheme depicted on a poster and accompanied by a detailed booklet is essential for arranging the information in a logical way and for guiding users in the selection of relevant information appropriate to their interests.

In the 'If I Were' series, 100 non-academic jobs are outlined in close-up leaflets, which consist of basic information, simply stated and designed to attract those pupils who are unlikely to take external examinations. A set of 20 can be bought for £1.

Career Outlines. In leaflet form again, these are wider in scope than the above and more educationally demanding, the intention being to broaden the student's understanding of different jobs to a point where he can consider if such a career is feasible in his particular case.

Career Specials. These consist generally of reprints of well written articles which have appeared in the careers press. Each article is selected because of the way it has shed new light on a particular job, though careers and appointments services in university and polytechnics are also covered.

Photoposters. These are, as the name suggests, a visual aid, each covering an area of work supplemented with a short text or suggested reading.

Sponsorships and Supplementary Awards. This is an annual publication costing £1.15, giving details of employers and professional bodies offering financial assistance to students following first degree, Higher National Diploma or comparable courses.

Catalogue of Careers Films. This is the most comprehensive publication of its type, listing those items which have been appraised by the Careers and Occupational Information Centre together with outside advisers. The list is not exhaustive, as it admits, but is nonetheless very useful and would be more so if revised on a regular basis.

The above comprise the main range of low-cost material available from the Centre. To this can be added a wealth of priced material, eg *Choice of Careers* booklets (presently being phased out), the 'Working in' series of well illustrated A4 sheets, *Close-ups* covering the different jobs available in any one industry and *Career Profiles* (to be sold and published by Nelson) which examine in depth different work available for people qualified in a particular occupational field. All are low-cost if considered as individual items, but when each series is considered as a whole the cost can be quite considerable, placing them outside the scope of this book. Finally, there is *COIC's Annual Careers Guide*.

Low-cost printed sources of information on higher education

There are in this field some essential texts which are undoubtedly expensive. On the other hand a considerable proportion of the information can be obtained free or at low cost, most of which deals with the questions often asked concerning higher education.

The Universities Central Council on Admissions (UCCA) issue free their *How to Apply for Admission to University*. This is as important for the students as the same organization's *Annual Report — Universities Central Council on Admissions* is for staff in recommending individual courses. The latter and the *Statistical Supplement* are available for less than £2.

Another important publication of relevance to universities is the *Compendium of Information for Entrance* (to the Scottish Universities), which gives entrance requirements in terms of Scottish Certificate of Education and General Certificate of Education examinations and lists all subjects which can be studied at undergraduate level at the Scottish universities.

The free *Leaflets (CH/1)* of Central Register and Clearing House Ltd give details of all degree and other advanced courses within the Central Register and Clearing House Scheme. This also includes details of all initial teacher education courses in England and Wales.

Important in its own field and of particular relevance to polytechnics is the free Council for National Academic Awards *Directory of First Degree and Diploma of Higher Education Courses*. This can be supplemented by the Polytechnics' own leaflets listing departments and courses.

Available as a low-cost item from the Regional Advisory Councils is a *Compendium of Advanced Courses in Colleges of Further and Higher Education*, listing all full- and part-time courses outside the universities.

Finally, the free publications of the Department of Education and Science include *Grants to Students: a brief guide*, which is an outline of the important financial considerations of further education, and *Courses in Agriculture, Horticulture and Forestry*, (National Consultative Committee for Agricultural Education), whilst a set of booklets in the 'Course Series' deals with major aspects of work, eg *Becoming an*

Engineer, Hotel and Catering, Tourism and Travel, Science at Work and *Using your Maths.*

Whereas a number of expensive publications cover in considerable depth details of individual further education establishments, their amenities as well as their courses, there is much to be said for collecting the institutions' own expensively produced *Prospectuses.* These are issued free to all schools with sixth forms and it is essential to be placed on their mailing lists.

Low-cost printed sources of information on jobs

The Careers Research and Advisory Centre (CRAC) publish a wide range of useful resources. An excellent publication, distributed free, is their annual *Job Book* which details approximately 4,000 training schemes in industry, commerce, hospitals and other public organizations, whilst the *Job Quiz Book* stimulates students to think more of their future by means of quizzes, puzzles, crosswords and teasers and in so doing should lead them to a more effective use of the occupational information in the school.

Valuable sources of further information are the Industrial Training Boards and numerous professional associations. The addresses of these are listed in the free booklet *Careers Information* by the Understanding British Industry Project (UBI). Compared with Cassell's *Careers Encyclopaedia*, the most comprehensive book of its type available, it is only half as extensive but the 200 addresses given make it easier to arrive at a useful selection of those worth contacting.

A quick and easy introduction to the world of careers is provided in *The Daily Telegraph's* low-cost publication *Careers A-Z*, which contains brief descriptions of a wide range of careers and occupations with information on entry and training requirements, and addresses.

Finally, to complete this section, a set of booklets published by the Central Services Unit for Universities and Polytechnics Careers and Appointments Services, which although conceived as a series, could be worth considering in terms of the individual titles. These encompass jobs to be found within various graduate disciplines such as geography or mechanical engineering. They represent good value and selected items, relevant to the needs of the school, are worth purchasing.

Periodicals

Free periodicals are available to cover most aspects of careers where currency is important. Those directly concerned with careers must surely be headed by the Careers and Occupational Information Centre's monthly *Newscheck*. This is very informative for staff in keeping up to date in three primary areas: in the field of new literature distributed by itself, new books and films; in current education and training; and in occupational and industrial news. All aspects and all levels of careers education and information are therefore covered whether applicable to less academic fifth formers or the high fliers in the sixth. The reviews of new resources by practitioners in the field are impartial and objective, and give a good indication as to what could be regarded as a high priority for the library. Also a system of coding the books received defines their level and scope, and potential readership. Other noteworthy features are news of future relevant television and radio programmes, new courses to be inaugurated, and the changes in address of professional and trade associations.

Employment News, the bi-monthly four-page newspaper of the Department of Employment, contains a vast amount of current information on training and job opportunities available through the various government-backed schemes and organizations. Other subjects included are new legislation affecting jobs, skill shortages, government policy, union news, health and safety at work, and the Economic Indicator's employment statistics and earnings levels. The paper attempts to present the information in an attractive way with the inclusion of black-and-white photographs, bold headlines and the occasional cartoon, but its readership will generally be confined to adults.

Focus is a periodical published three times per annum by the Committee of Directors of Polytechnics, and as such is invaluable in informing potential students of the courses offered in the various institutions. The articles are readable and well illustrated with black-and-white photographs, often identifying individual students, who are able to offer their comments, and the projects they are undertaking as part of their course. New courses at the polytechnics are also reviewed in depth.

Which Course?, the monthly journal for Higher Education and Training, is a commercially produced publication financed by the advertising of education institutions. Articles on particular areas of work are written by well qualified individuals who, the editor says, have a completely free hand to express their own views. Alongside each article courses, relevant to that area of work, are advertised.

Rethink—a course or a job or both, a periodical in substantial newspaper format, is published each summer by the Careers Research and Advisory Centre and aims to present coherently the options in higher education open to students. It includes a useful course and careers guides index enabling the student to direct his interest through further education in a logical fashion. Other areas covered include grants, re-sitting examinations, taking a year off, sponsorship and adapting to college life. The information is well organized and presented attractively with examples of students already involved in further education with which the sixth former may be able to identify. As with *Which Course?*, the advertising of numerous institutions is found on virtually every page, each one competing with the other. One must assume the individual uses his own judgement in coming to any conclusion before committing himself to any one institution. However, the sixth form careers tutors, if not the counselling of the Further Education Information Service run by each local authority, which is given some prominence in the paper, and the fact that it is published by the Careers Research and Advisory Centre, should overcome any major weaknesses or doubts in this respect.

Away from the specific publications directly concerned with careers are a number of useful periodicals which could serve to increase pupils' awareness and stimulate interest in different kinds of jobs and industries. A comprehensive list of free and low-cost journals will be found in Appendix 3, but it is of value to highlight those of possible use in the careers field. They are generally published by the giants in both the private and public sectors, offer employment to millions and provide excellent career prospects: sound justification enough for their inclusion in the library.

First of all are the various armed forces journals: *Navy News*, representing the Royal Navy, *Globe and Laurel*, the Marines, and *Flight Deck*, the Fleet Air Arm. The role of the Army is conveyed in *Soldier*, whilst the interaction of the various services is covered in *Nato Review*. All are attractively produced magazines and give a good indication of the day to day life of service personnel, their various roles, skills and satisfactions.

Project, a magazine about engineering for young people, prepared for the Industry Education Advisory Committee by the Central Office of Information, is excellent for inculcating in sixth formers the vital role of engineering in the economy and thus as a possible career. A behind-the-scenes look at important processes in industry is covered in well illustrated and tightly written articles each written by eminent contributors. The work of different kinds of engineers, prominent engineers of the past and the latest engineering developments are also included.

The work of engineers in specific industries is also covered in such periodicals as *British Telecom Journal*, a quality publication with full colour illustrations, maps and diagrams; *Atom*, representing the United Kingdom Atomic Energy Authority, a heavyweight journal but important for covering the world of this energy source; *Ford News*, the house journal of the firm and the most representative of the automobile industry.

The oil industry is encompassed in *Shell Education News* and *Esso*

Magazine. The former is aimed more at the teaching staff and often contains details of the kind of work available and more especially sponsorship of students. *Esso Magazine* on the other hand has some excellent articles on all aspects of the oil industry.

Finally, two periodicals which might increase students' awareness of Voluntary Services Overseas; *Bother*, a monthly commentary on poverty and the struggle for development produced by Oxfam, and *Development News*, published monthly by the Foreign and Commonwealth Office.

Newspapers

The two most important are the Monday edition of *The Daily Telegraph* and *The Observer.*

The Daily Telegraph offers a Careers and Information Service whereby a student is able to contact the paper for advice, the only cost being a stamped addressed envelope. The paper's regular article on careers is well researched and topical—for instance covering new regulations for entry to a particular profession, and always contains sources of further information. The paper has become an authority in the field of careers by publishing a range of material on the subject, one item of which, *Careers A-Z*, has already been mentioned as being available at low cost.

The Observer, in its Business Section, has a regular article on careers which is supplemented with the issue of free leaflets for those who request them on the particular job covered that week. One major feature of the articles is the study of any recent report or legislation affecting the job market.

Films

The Careers and Occupational Information Centre make freely available their *Catalogue of Careers Films*, the most recent edition being, however, dated 1980. This identifies over 100 free titles available from a number of sources—or approximately one quarter of the films listed. For each film there is a critical synopsis which enables the selector to gain a good impression of the content in order to decide whether or not it would be relevant to the audience in question. This is especially useful as in the distributor's own catalogue the description of films is often inadequate or even misleading. The catalogue can be updated to some extent throughout the year by *Newscheck* which mentions certain new releases. Some films can, in fact, appear in the distributor's own catalogues months before the Centre reviews them, if in fact it ever does so. (It might be worth reiterating that the Careers and Occupational Information Centre accepts that the list is by no means exhaustive, a point to be covered later.) The catalogue does, however, provide a more than adequate indication of the useful free items available on most aspects of careers and can be regarded as the best source listing most of the films from such organizations as professional associations, training boards and education institutions which act as their own distributors, a fact generally not realized. Most important of its omissions include a number of useful titles from Barclays Bank, British Gas, the Electricity Council and Golden Films (Viscom), a free film library representing some major companies. This should emphasize the need for the school to have available the widest range of film catalogues for consultation so that a number of staff planning a film programme for, say, a careers week, can make the best possible selection. There are also the excellent free publications of some individual organizations which produce comprehensive lists of films available in their area. A first class example of this is the *RIBA Directory of Films*, an annotated list of 125 films with an architectural interest from 50 distributors. Thirty-two of the films are listed as free. Another example is that entitled *A Series of Films from PETT* (Project Engineers and Technology for Tomorrow). All the 19 films listed here are free. Undoubtedly the most useful source of information about a specific field is the appropriate professional body or specialist organization and these are dealt with in the final part of this section.

Free literature

This includes leaflets, booklets and posters on careers or more specially the jobs themselves. In general the information available is well produced, comprehensive and accurate, coming as it does from primary sources. Another point in its favour is its currency—especially useful for salaries; it is authoritative, listing relevant courses and qualifications, together with details of exemptions, and the associated colleges and the fact that the information can be obtained in multiple copies, convenient for distribution to interested pupils who will benefit by being able to retain it and peruse it at their leisure, and amongst friends.

The sources of literature fall into four broad groups, each of which will be considered in turn.

Public bodies. These include the civil and local government services, the nationalized industries and the armed forces, each providing copious literature of all kinds detailing individual occupations within the main organizations. For instance the Civil Service provides booklets, each of 40 pages, on the different professions it employs; economists, engineers, lawyers, scientists and the like, all of which are covered in depth, whilst other less responsible jobs are included in coloured leaflets such as *Come*

Typing: Civil Service careers 1979. General information is covered in other publications such as *Civil Service Jobs—where to find out more—Regional Advisers, and Government Departments Appointment Executive and Clerical Officers,* a booklet to help candidates for Executive Officer and Clerical Officer posts choose where they would prefer to work.

Nationalized industries also produce literature. For example, the National Bus Company draws attention to the various jobs available, in a colourful leaflet—*A National Career with the Biggest Bus and Coach Company in the World.* Details of specific jobs are examined in a booklet, such as *Executive Courses in Road Passenger Transport Management.* Background information is available on the industry or service, for example *The Story of National Buses, a History,* while *Function, Organising and Capability* would enable the student to see a possible career in transport in perspective.

The armed forces, through their local Career Offices, supplemented by individual publications from the Ministry of Defence, provide an excellent range of lavishly produced material detailing all aspects of the Services.

Industrial Training Boards. The 10 boards represent a wide cross-section of the industrial community. The information they provide is not extensive, considering the labour force within their purview, but what is available is usually just one basic leaflet or booklet (in multiple copies) which defines succinctly the kind of work available, the qualifications required and where they can be studied. Other sources of further information and advice are given, especially employers' organizations, who can supply information on companies which might be located in the area. A representative example of this literature is *Careers in Hotels and Catering for People Who Like People.*

Professional associations. While all these organizations have some material available on their respective profession, it will generally consist of no more than two different kinds of leaflets, one on the role of the institution, the other on the qualifications or course exemptions required to join it. One has, therefore, the Association of Certified Accountants with their *Put Yourself in a Winning Position—a graduate career as a Certified Accountant* and *Examination Regulations and Qualifications for Membership; Certified Accountant,* or the Royal Institute of Chartered Surveyors with its *Academic Standards of Entry* and *A Career as a Chartered Surveyor.* The information is sufficient to enlighten the student without going into too great a depth and on the whole is presented in an impartial way with little embellishment over and above basic facts. If anything, the information is presented in too staid and dry a manner, perhaps in keeping with their image. A list of the principal associations can be found in the Understanding British Industry publication *Careers Information*.

Private concerns. In contrast to the above group, companies, especially the multinationals whose advertisements and addresses are readily found in the newspapers, are capable of producing the most exotic literature, usually in the form of glossy booklets up to 50 pages long, replete with colour illustrations, diagrams, maps, statistics and of course a text extolling the worth of the firm in terms of career prospects. Students should be able to see at first hand the practical application of qualifications to a work situation especially when reading case histories of employees graphically portrayed in the literature. The wide scope commerce and industry have to offer is certainly emphasized. Information on local firms can invariably be obtained from the local careers office.

All told, the literature can become quite a substantial part of the library by taking up a corner of it, increasing pupils' awareness of jobs and further education by its accessibility, acting as a valuable source of reference and generally providing useful reading matter over and above its inherent utilitarian value. For instance, material on such topics as nursing, secretarial work, hairdressing, the Merchant Navy, the police and the armed forces have a perennial interest for pupils, even though only a minority eventually pursue any one career.

Another important aspect of the literature is the interesting and useful work it can provide for students who can be delegated jobs in the acquiring and organizing of the information. The writing of letters, maintaining a card index of sources, classifying and filing, are just some of the skills involved, all of which encourage a thorough and logical approach to work.

Environmental Studies

This subject is relatively new to the curriculum, and as such, its content is difficult to determine; it depends on how it is taught in the individual school—whether in fact it is regarded as a subject in its own right or as an adjunct to another, be it history, geography, biology or general studies. The emphasis the school places on it, therefore, determines the academic content and amount of material required, perhaps as much in this subject as in any. Key topics in environmental studies can, however, be identified and these will have relevance in most schools, no matter how the subject is taught. These will be given due emphasis later, but first of all a general impression of the resources themselves.

An excellent article by Stephen Sterling which appeared in *The Times Educational Supplement* on 4 July 1981,[1] showed that there is a tremendous amount of resource material available in this field. The author also pointed out some of the problems, such as the fact that important organizations in the field have similar names as well as similar roles.

First of all, it is useful to look at the key organizations.

The professional body for teachers involved in this subject is the National Association for Environmental Education (NAEE). All its publications are available at low-cost, regardless of whether the school has a current subscription. If the school does subscribe to the Association, then there is a discount on the material which includes direct mailings of the twice-yearly journal *Environmental Education*, three *Newsletters* and copious information on current published literature, from which it is possible to assess those publications of most value. The journal brings together current news, ideas from practising educationalists and details of new teaching aids, including those at low-cost.

In the summer edition of 1980 there was, for example, a critical review of teaching aids on the topic of energy from both commercial and non-commercial sources, with due emphasis being placed on value for money with a number of low-cost items being recommended. Back numbers of the journal can be obtained for reference.

One of the key publications from the National Association for Environmental Education is *Environmental Education—a statement of aims*, setting out the objectives of environmental education, in detail, at all levels. This is regarded as the only definitive statement on the subject and is a must for those planning new courses and developing Mode Three papers, as well as for creating integrated schemes of work in the middle school years.

Other specific publications are available to help staff plan courses, Mode One or Three Certificate of Secondary Education and General Certificate of Education 'O' and 'A' level. These include practical guides on aviaries, greenhouses, aquariums and incubators in schools, and organizing visits outside the classroom.

Another important organization is the Town and Country Planning Association which specializes in the urban environment though other ecological problems are also covered from time to time. Through the medium of its monthly journal *BEE* (Bulletin of Environmental Education), much useful material is made available, from guides to sources and resources; special pull-out supplements; teaching ideas and materials and authoritative articles through to actual reprints of articles from newspapers and the technical press which have teaching potential, or which bridge the gap between the environmentalist and the teaching profession. Without a doubt *BEE* can act as a catalyst in stimulating new ideas to be taken further in the classroom. Taking an issue of the Bulletin at random, that of May 1978, *BEE 85*, the contributors include the Director of Heritage Education Year, the Director of the Countryside Education Trust, a headmaster, the Education Officer of the Directorate of Ancient Monuments and Historic Buildings and the Director of Youth National Trust Theatre, as well as teachers and other practising educationalists. With such a broad span of relevant intellectual backgrounds, the articles convey a fairly accurate picture of current environmental issues. Off-prints of all key articles from *BEE* are available at low–cost and, though lacking an index, the contents of back issues are tabulated for easy reference. It is also possible to buy back issues, either singly or in bound form for a particular year.

Finally to those special pull-out resources supplements of *BEE*. As there is so much material from all different kinds of sources as well as of all types, no special coverage is given to low-cost items, though they do appear in the lists. The material, usually on one key environmental issue such as pollution, water, urban ecology, new towns or human settlements, is listed according to type, whether in the form of books, films, wallcharts, etc. Annotations are brief and uncritical, though details of costs are given.

To fulfil these aims it has produced a low-cost source book, a *Guide to Resources in Environmental Education*. This is published annually, making the information as up to date as is feasible in this field, and is altogether very comprehensive. All the material is appraised in a brief but critical way and includes books, an excellent index of useful articles from 27 of the periodicals in this subject; study kits, films, wallcharts, future radio and television programmes and over 50 names and addresses of organizations active in educational environmental matters. It is of interest to note that the Trust operates a Resource Bank, perhaps the most comprehensive of its type, and includes in it virtually all the material appearing in its Guide, as well as much more. For a small fee schools are able to borrow these resources by post.

The Trust publishes a termly newsletter which gives details of new educational material available, both from itself and from other sources. Exhibitions can be arranged, at low cost, of the material held by the Trust and this can be an excellent way of assessing at first hand a wide range of resources. These can also be supplemented by a speaker, again another low-cost service.

Current publications of the Trust are wide-ranging, covering the whole aspect of the environment and nearly all are low–cost. First of all there are short sets of notes suitable for use by teachers in lesson preparation, and by pupils for projects. These cover all the key areas such as pollution, ecology, population, energy and wildlife conservation. In order that these can be incorporated in the curriculum in the best possible way, short guides are available for teachers giving practical advice on tried and tested schemes. Next there are more in-depth publications, again on important issues, and aimed at the more academic student. Examples include: *European Environment 1975–2000* —a simulation lasting 100 minutes which enables the sixth former to consider the possible environmental consequences of the enlarged European Economic Community by the turn of the century; *Using the Local Environment* is designed to encourage practical work in the area around the school and includes a supplement on suggested local survey work, while *The Economic Transition* puts economic growth in historical perspective, showing it to be a mere transitional phase between different steady states.

It is appropriate to mention at this time the resources of the Conservation Society (founded to make people more aware of the effects on our environment of the population explosion and the unwise use of technology), a sister organization of the Conservation Trust. Although both organizations do, to some extent, collaborate on educational matters, they do publish certain material independently. In fact the Society has a vigorous publishing policy in its own right mainly due, perhaps, to its many working parties on education, transport, pollution, land use, population and energy. Numerous publications are free for the asking and reflect the strong views of this pressure group. Titles include *Nuclear Power—salvation or death trap?*; *Roads to Ruins* and *Do We Need the Heavy Lorry?* Others at low-cost spell out at greater length specific policies on population growth, conservation and transport. All are well argued statements backed up with facts, and can serve to stimulate students to think of the future, and not to accept things as they are. Excellent titles here would be *Test Your Survival Score* and *Crisis of Lifestyles*. Finally the Society publishes in a popular newspaper format *Good Earth*, and *Conservation News.*

The last major organization to be dealt with as a source of information on environmental studies is the Council for Environmental Education (CEE), a charitable institution, based at the School of Education, University of Reading, and financed principally by the Department of the Environment and local education authorities who subscribe to its publications. The Council's field of interest is not limited to the rural elements of the environment as it recognizes that the urban and rural elements of the environment are inextricably linked and interdependent. The Council, therefore, has a strong institutional base and this, combined with its broad policy, makes it perhaps the most useful and authoritative of organizations in environmental education.

Bearing this in mind, it is not surprising to find that the Council for Environmental Education has taken on a co-ordinating role, bringing together interested bodies in the need to disseminate information, the result being an excellent publication, *Environmental Education Enquiries,* produced in conjunction with the aforementioned Conservation Trust. This lists 250 environmental organizations with advice on the type of help available in 16 major areas. The need for such a publication is reflected in the fact that an extended version of this booklet has been published by the Department of Education and Science: *DES Environmental Education Sources of Information 1981.*

The usefulness of *Environmental Education Enquiries* lies in the fact that it brings together 180 organizations, all of which in some way can provide material of use to schools. These are listed alphabetically with their addresses and details of the services they can provide. There is also a classification of organizations by topics, 25 in all, enabling the inquirer to see at a glance which are the most relevant sources for any one particular subject. The information on each organization is comprehensive, providing such details as whether it is a recommended source or not, whether the material provided is only suitable for more advanced work, and whether there are catalogues or information sheets available. However, details of costs (if any) or titles of individual publications are not given. The strength, of course, is in its ease of use, enabling one to assess generally what material is available, an exceedingly important item in planning a course or when a change in the curriculum demands fresh resources.

For more detailed information, it is necessary to examine the Council's *Directory of Environmental Literature and Teaching Aids.* This publication is divided into sections according to type of material—films, teaching aids (including posters, study kits, games and work cards) and magazines, all of which contain numerous items at low-cost. The extra detail given here extends to naming items and costs involved (if any) as well as, in some cases, stating where it best may be used. In each category of material the organizations are listed alphabetically so the reader will have to scan the lists in order to ascertain what will be relevant to his needs. This publication is, of course, best used in conjunction with *Environmental Education Enquiries.*

Obviously in an area such as environmental studies, where numerous organizations are only too keen to supply teaching materials, and where some topics are more important than others as far as most schools are concerned, it is not surprising to find that the Council for Environmental Education has produced some separate low-cost 'Resource Sheets' on finding out about specific aspects on the subject. These number seven in all and include such titles as *Farming and the Rural Environment, Nuclear Energy* and *Nature in the Town*. Taking as an example *Materials and Sources of Information on Pollution*, this begins with an introduction to the subject, then continues with flow diagrams dealing with a comparison of natural and man-made processes. A list of recommended books follows, then specific magazine articles and leaflets that are primarily free or low–cost—over 30 in all, from a number of sources, enough, in fact, to give a balanced picture. After these are posters—again low–cost, then kits and project ideas. As a conclusion, there is a list of 11 organizations which are willing to help with individual enquiries.

Before leaving the Council for Environmental Education, those low-cost publications which are teaching resources themselves should be mentioned. These range from booklets on the teaching of environmental studies and curriculum planning to field work guides and identification booklets on plants. Finally there is the termly journal *Review of Environmental Education* (REED), containing articles, news and reviews of interest to all who are involved in this subject at any level, and the monthly *Newsheet* providing above all details of new publications and teaching aids with many at low–cost.

The work of these four organizations has done much to control information about the resources available in environmental studies. However, in order to assess the situation still further, a closer look at specific material in terms of its use in the classroom is worthwhile. This will be followed by an examination of specific types of material of general use.

Purely for theoretical purposes it is possible to categorize the resources under three main topic headings:

a. The urban environment.
b. The rural environment.
c. The international environment.

(a) *The urban environment*

Top of the list here is the Civic Trust and its offshoot, Heritage Education Group, which was created by the Department of the Environment. The Group's aim is to stimulate the study of the urban environment and our historic heritage at all levels of education. Paramount in its success has been its ability to bring together the world of the planners and education. *Civic Trust News* and *Heritage Education News* are the principal publications disseminating current information on the urban scene. Books have been published, too, including *Education and Heritage, The Young Environmentalist* and *Environment and the Community*; this last deals with the practical implications of carrying out a major project on a town.

Similar material is available from Community Service Volunteers in such publications as their *Planning Your Environment* which contains many suggestions for projects on the local environment and how best it can be improved.

Other sections deal with who's who in local government, getting to know your town, finding communities, improving your neighbourhood, the ecology of the city, projects and resources.

Youth Environmental Action is also able to assist those who want to do something to improve or protect their environment. It can also provide advice and information on environmental issues and action as outlined in its series of publications called *Fact and Action Guides*.

On the subject of transport the British Road Federation can help with such titles as *Roads in Towns*, *British Road Programmes* and *Motorway Progress*. Providing alternative views on the subject is Transport 2000 with its publications. On the other hand the Department of the Environment has publications available such as *Transport and the Environment* which presents the facts in perhaps a more balanced way.

(b) *The rural environment*

For an overall picture of natural habitats, the Nature Conservancy Council has a large selection of material available as well as details of other sources in its Mail Order Catalogue. A number of items are free or low-cost. Its own material includes details on its own work covered principally in its annual reports, nature conservation in general, reserves, policy statements and habitats, of particular note are the agriculture and wildlife leaflets with such self-explanatory titles as *Wildlife and Farmland*, *Hedges and Shelterbelts*, *Pesticides* and *Tree Planting* and *Wildlife Conservation*.

At low-cost is *Agricultural Chemicals and Wildlife*. This project, using maps and diagrams, includes a review of the effects of chemicals on wildlife, questions for students to answer, suggestions for field work and relevant leaflets and further references that can be followed up. Reproduction of this material is allowed for classroom use. Various wallcharts are also available at low-cost on habitats—oak woods, lowland farmland, sand dunes, salt marshes and wet lands. The Conservancy's *Information Sheet 1* on resources other than its own, identifies a number of low-cost items from such diverse sources as the Society for Promotion of Nature Conservation, Friends of the Earth, Pedigree Pet Foods, Universities Federation for Animal Welfare, Scottish Home and Health Department and *The Sunday Telegraph*. Finally the Nature Conservancy publishes two free journals—*Naturopa*, at rather irregular intervals and the monthly *Nature Newsletter.*

The Council for Nature, an amalgamation of many august natural history and conservation bodies such as the British Trust for Ornithology, the Royal Society for the Protection of Birds and the Zoological Society of London, is an active low-cost publisher of educational material. Outstanding among these are the booklets *School Grounds: a resource for teaching and environmental studies; Predatory Mammals in Britain* and *Wild Birds and the Law;* posters on endangered flowers, plants and animals and its journal *Habitat* published 10 times per year, containing news from national wildlife organizations.

Two further organizations worth noting are the Fauna Preservation Society, involved with the saving of rare creatures worldwide, especially important since the World Wildlife Fund reduced its educational resources in 1980, and the Botanical Society of the British Isles. Neither, it must be said, produces a plethora of low-cost material, but for specific information or advice on their respective subjects they can prove indispensible.

(c) *The international environment*

There are numerous organizations, both large and small, active in monitoring and putting forward their own views on and offering panacea for the world's inexorable consumption of natural resources. All provide a wide selection of free and low-cost material suitable for use in schools. Perhaps the leader in this respect is Friends of the Earth. Its publications are well researched and usually receive excellent reviews from the quality press. Principal topic areas covered include future energy needs, food consumption and transport. Good examples on these subjects are *The Fissile Society* on the social and financial implications of centralized electricity generators, *Nuclear Prospects* dealing with the problems of security and the resultant loss of freedom of the individual if greater use of nuclear energy goes ahead; *Changing Food Habits in the UK,* an assessment of the social, technological, economic and political factors which influence dietary patterns and *Wastage in the UK Food System*—an analysis of the flow of food in the United Kingdom and of the losses incurred within the system. On transport, the *Politics of Urban Transport Planning* is an analysis of transport policy formulated and the factors which influence the decision making process.

The Environmental Group Information Service (EGIS) publishes a number of teaching aids as well as a magazine on such topics as new food crops, oil consumption worldwide, including current spillages, transport and waste. The teaching aids include education packs with such titles as *An Introduction to Waste Pollution, Energy Resources* and *World Food Prospects*—which looks at the world food situation and what it means to the United Kingdom. The information ranges from traditional systems of production to new protein alternatives as well as looking carefully at the question of pesticide usage, processing and economics.

The problems of the Third World are now regarded as an area within the orbit of environmental studies and here, perhaps, the most important organization is Oxfam. Recent material it has published includes *Pictorial Discussion Sheets* on such subjects as population, water and poverty.

Another aspect of the broadening field of environmental education is its closer involvement with political theory, well illustrated with such organizations as the Socialist Environment and Resources Association (SERA), or the Green Alliance. Both have low-cost publications of interest. The first has *Ecosocialism in a Nutshell* illustrating with strip cartoons the so-called ecological perspective whilst the second group has published two pamphlets dealing with the historical process which has cumulated in the consumer economy, where the system of values leaves environmental factors low on the list of priorities.

Covering the whole field of possible future energy sources and, ultimately, life styles, is the material of the National Centre for Alternative Technology. This ranges from information sheets on possible energy saving systems such as community recycling and wind power utilization through to a survey on energy possibilities by the year 2025, using coal and ambient energy systems, and ultimately to an *Energy Pack*. The pack has been designed for anyone wanting to gain an understanding of existing energy use and alternative energy sources. Designed particularly with teachers in mind, it consists of six sections with information sheets, plans, posters, points for discussion, details of working systems and sources of information. Though not available at low-cost, it is well worth considering as the Centre's reputation is second to none in this field.

Another excellent source on this subject is the Shell Briefing Service with such material as *Energy Profile*—data displayed in various formats. A number of the large oil companies are actively involved in research into new forms of energy, so are worth approaching for information.

Finally, to place the environmentalist's considerations in a realistic context, the European Commission has published two free relevant documents—*The European Commission Environment Policy* and *The European Commission and the Energy Problem*.

Periodicals

Besides the journals, newsletters and bulletins of the organizations mentioned, much material on the environment can be gutted from newspapers on a day-to-day basis, whether concerned with oil slicks, new technology, aiding the energy situation, the demolition of listed buildings, open cast coal sites, new transport systems and the introduction of heavier lorries to Britain's roads. In-depth articles often appear in *The Observer, The Guardian* and *The Sunday Times*; the last named also prints a series called 'Watch', the children's and young teenagers' environmental club, highlighting current issues.

Environmental issues within the Common Market appear in *Euroforum*, the free journal from the information section of the Commission of the European Communities. As an example, in the December 1980 issue, relevant subjects covered included the use of tidal power as an energy source, the siting of nuclear plants and the side effects of new technologies.

Films

Early in 1980 the Department of Town and Country Planning of the University of Manchester published its *Urban and Environmental Studies: a film guide*, providing an abstract of 550 titles available on free loan or hire, having recognized that this medium was not widely known amongst educationalists or the environment professions. It was also thought, based on the reasoning of a Department of the Environment Report, that in terms of teaching materials, films were very important as a basis for both information and critical debate. It is gratifying, therefore, to find that a considerable number of them, covering most aspects of the environment, are free.

The Council for Environmental Education's *Directory of Environmental Literature and Teaching Aids* (DELTA), also itemizes a useful collection of films, not as many as in the former case, but each has a more detailed abstract. The films in both cases are found under classified headings, 11 in the first instance and 20 in the second, which, despite the fewer entries, does make it easier to locate those relevant to one's needs and hence is the more practical publication.

Neither directory claims to be exhaustive though they are both as up to date as one gets in this field. As far as films relevant to this book are concerned, the second publication is able to offer a wider selection.

The dissimilar classification, amounting to arbitrary groupings, emphasizes the difficulty in coming to any conclusion in arriving at a successful arrangement of the material. Bearing this in mind, the following assessment of the free films will be done by examining them from the point of view of distributor/source which, in general, dictates their content anyway.

The multinationals, especially the oil companies, are able to offer films on a broad aspect of environmental issues. *Environment in the Balance*, released by Shell, shows how geological, topographical and social development in Britain have helped to shape its environment and discusses the problems of industrial expansion, population growth and pollution. Dealing with pollution in rivers is *The River Must Live*, which emphasizes the consequences when water courses are overloaded with waste, and the action required to keep them pure. This theme is explored still further in *The Threat in the Water*, and is concerned with the killer diseases known as Bilharzia which affects 200 million people throughout the arid regions of the world and is contracted from pollutants.

Back to this country, ICI has produced a film called *The Choice*, describing what has been done to combat pollution of all kinds to our air, water and land.

Particular aspects of aerial pollution at a large chemical complex are shown in *Something to Sing About* where it was possible to eradicate massive amounts of pollution, though at a heavy cost in financial terms. ICI also has a useful range of films on how pesticides and herbicides are made and what is done to check that they are environmentally safe with such titles as *Life in the Balance* and *A Way with Weeds*. The need to farm more intensively in order to feed an ever-growing population is outlined in *The Precious Soil*. The justification for artificial pesticides and fertilizers is also discussed in Shell's *Pesticides in Focus* and *The Land Must Provide*, in a world where population and the demand for food are ever increasing and where alternative methods of increasing yields are inadequate.

On farming systems in this country, the National Farmers Union has two films—*Look to the Land* and *Look to the Hills*, which both seek to show how modern methods can be integrated into the landscape and yet produce greater yields. On the other hand, the Royal Society for the Prevention of Cruelty to Animals has two films on factory farming with *To Live Like a Pig* and *Egg Machine*.

On a lighter note are the series of films from Shell on six regions of Britain noted for their beauty where the natural environment is at its best. The factors responsible are examined and discussed.

This aspect of the natural environment is also covered in various titles of National's library. These include *Beauty in Trust* on the work of the National Trust, *The Changing Forest* on the Forestry Commission, with its efforts at land conservation and preservation, *The Living Pattern* on the work of the Nature Conservancy, and *People and Season*, where the greater mobility and rising living standards of the population are discussed in context with their impact on the countryside.

Another important area where the environment is under threat is that from energy sources, and here there are a number of relevant films, most notably from the Central Electricity Generating Board (CEGB) and the Gas Council. Covering the general implications of energy are films such as *Research for Power*, describing the experimental research programme into efficient electrical systems, and *Energy in Perspective*, which discusses man's historic use of energy and examines the limits of the world's supply of fossil fuels alongside alternative sources, such as nuclear, solar, tidal and geothermal power.

Perhaps the role of nuclear power has posed the biggest question for environmentalists and this is given full coverage in such films as *Energy—the Nuclear Option*, *BNFL at the Heart of Nuclear Power* and *Nuclear Generation*. As yet there are no free films showing the opposing arguments.

Gas as an energy source is well illustrated in *Too Good to Waste*, showing how man has wasted valuable and irreplaceable fuel, but with the introduction of North Sea gas, effective systems minimize losses, and *Britain's Natural Gas*—a general interest documentary on the fuel. Following on from the actual production of this major energy source is the distribution network involved and how its possible effects on the environment can be minimized. *Below the Line* and *Good Neighbours* show what the Central Electricity Generating Board has done to preserve the countryside where power lines have been constructed. In the case of British Gas, such films as *Harvest, Caledonian Pipeline* and *Living with Gas* have much the same story to tell with areas disturbed by pipe laying yielding high quality produce soon afterwards.

The National Coal Board has also produced films of interest to environmental studies dealing with effective production methods and site reclamation. *Tomorrow's Coal* examines the Selby coalfield with all its implications; *Using the Coal* suggests purposes to which coal may be extended towards the end of this century, whilst *Restoration of Land after Open Cast Coalmining* and *Case History—Redcar and Coldrife* show how, in two cases, the countryside can be made good again, firstly for agricultural purposes and secondly for recreation use respectively.

Other topics within the environmental field have also been produced by British Gas and the Central Electricity Generating Board. *The Seas Around Us* examines the marine environment when fish stocks are dwindling, whilst *The Air—my enemy* looks at air contamination and research into better ways of using fuel as well as commentary on social factors such as human greed.

The Central Electricity Generating Board has also produced some films on natural history on such themes as salmon, a nature trail around a power station and one of special note about the countryside, presented by Phil Drabble, illustrating the balance between industry and nature.

The conservation of wildlife can be taken a step further by examining what is being done in various countries through the world by making use of those films available from embassies and other institutions representing national interests. Films such as *The Catch* on the relocation of caribou in Canada, *The Wild are Free* on the Kruger National Park, and *Wyperfield*, an Australian sanctuary, are good examples. Other countries with good useful material include Sweden, Finland, Poland, West Germany, India and Japan.

Finally to the free films of the Central Film Library, which relate mainly to the urban environment. The topics covered include the new towns, water consumption, rubbish and conservation and renovation of old towns. Examples include *Spot the Difference*, encouraging pupils to look at their built environment, and *Rubbish Tips*, featuring Ronnie Barker as Director of the rubbish, enlisting the help of volunteers to clean up the neighbourhood.

REFERENCES

1   Sterling, Stephen   'Resources for Courses', *The Times Educational Supplement* 4 July 1980. 33-44.

General Studies and Contemporary Problems

This subject, as its name suggests, is an amalgam of academic disciplines taught within the school, with the addition of modern problems and current affairs, and these will be the main concern of this section. For students to attain a high standard in it, they must be widely read, not only because the syllabus is so broad, but because there are no set text books. By watching television selectively, listening to radio documentaries and reading a quality daily newspaper, an individual can go a long way to imbibing a sufficiency of knowledge in this subject, and here the library can obviously help. But more in-depth material is necessary for any structured course when students are required to write essays on selected areas that interest them.

A good deal of useful material can be obtained for the library at low-cost, though it must be said there are no substitutes for such publications as a current encyclopaedia or *Keesings Archives.*

First and foremost there are newspapers, both the Sunday papers with their colour supplements and the quality dailies. The potential of this medium lies in the way relevant articles can be taken out and filed away for reference purposes. Perennial topics would include British politics, the European Economic Community, the Third World, China, South Africa, Russia, communism, women's liberation, health, social problems (housing, homelessness, welfare rights, the old and the sick), defence, education, energy, censorship, the economy, race (community relations), local government, freedom, prisons, Northern Ireland, American politics and current problems of concern, such as the Iranian situation, El Salvador, the Polish issue and the fishing industry. The best information is that appearing in in-depth reports rather than in straight news items and the most useful examples are to be found in *The Sunday Times*, *The Observer* and *The Guardian*. In order to demonstrate the usefulness of this material it is of value to highlight examples. The Sunday supplements are invaluable here for their inclusion of excellent colour illustrations accompanying the usually well researched articles.

The Sunday Times

Of possible perennial interest are 'The survivors' (22.2.81), dealing with a visit to the atom bombed cities of Nagasaki and Hiroshima, seen against the background of a visit by Pope John Paul II; the 'Super spy' (8.2.81), on the extent of South Africa's spying activities; 'Poland—living next to the Bear' (18.1.81), a survey of the unrest in this country and placing it in a historic perspective, drawing its strength from Roman Catholicism and a perennial desire for national independence, while 'The Imprisonment of Lech Walesa' (31.10.82) continues on the same theme. 'The island they killed' (15.2.81), shows that after 40 years, a Scottish island is still contaminated from the effects of a chemical warfare experiment. 'The 79-billion dollar menace' (22.8.82), highlights the drug problem in the United States; while problems of a different nature, that of juvenile delinquency in China, are covered by 'Doing time in China' (9.1.83). Two topics of interest pertaining to Britain—politics and the media, and the National Health Service appear in the following two articles, 'Politicians for sale' (8.5.83) and 'Is medicine sick' (11.9.83). Internal strife within countries is often the subject of articles, an example being 'The Longest War' (7.8.83) on the Eritrea problem.

The Observer

'The amazing Ernie' (1.3.81), is a critical biography written by the producer of an Independent Television documentary on the same subject about Ernest Bevan; the determination of Brazilian Indians to resist the inroads of civilization into the Amazon Basin is covered in 'The tribes that won't surrender' (25.1.81); 'The Rising Sun shines in the valleys' (26.4.81) deals with the establishment of Japanese firms in Wales, while in the same issue is an article on conservation—'Moving houses', which shows that a successful way to preserve old buildings is to dismantle them piecemeal and re-erect them elsewhere.

On the international front 'Russia—watchers of the Arctic ice' (15.5.83), 'Warriors of the Deep' (22.5.83), and 'How they buried Leonid

Ilyich Brezhnev' (28.11.82) reflect on East/West relations. The ramifications of the nuclear issue at home can be studied in 'Women at the wire' (12.12.82). Other examples of major conflicts which have been covered are 'Beirut: after the massacre' (5.12.82), and 'The war the world forgot', referring to the Iran-Iraq war. 'Pinochet's Chile' (4.9.83) covers the internal conflict found within the country. Much nearer home on a more mundane level is the 'Doleful years' (8.5.83), an illustrated examination of how government policies have affected jobs and industry in Britain in the last four years.

The Sunday Telegraph

Problems associated with the increasing strength of Russia's navy are examined in 'The fierce race for sea power' (15.2.81); on a similar theme of survival in an inhospitable world is 'Ready for Domesday' (11.1.81); assuming man survives, then future lifestyles, as in 'Buildings growing under the sea' (1.1.81) could be a worthwhile proposition, while, in the same issue, the problems of the ape species and how they have learned to adjust to ecological changes is shown in 'Learning from the gorillas'.

The subject of military strength is taken up in 'Sitting on defence' (1.5.83), a profile of Michael Heseltine; 'Righting wrongs in Europe' (6.3.83), deals with a look at the European Court of Human Rights whilst 'How do opinion polls work' is the subject of an article in 5.6.83.

The Guardian

The Guardian has two regular series of significance, each appearing weekly. The first is 'Futures, the world of science and technology' which often extends to two or more pages in length and includes a correspondence section, thus encouraging feedback and open discussion on often controversial issues. Contributors are usually eminent scientists, while the articles themselves may be extracts from recently published or forthcoming books, or international conferences. Bibliographies or references to further reading are frequently given.

The range of subjects covered is vast and as many of the articles are dealing with the frontiers of science involving both social and technological factors, individual topics are difficult to categorize. A pattern can be distinguished, however, and there are articles on subjects of general interest such as scientific co-operation on an international basis with the inherent political conditions, lifestyles of the future and changes affected by technology on our industrial infrastructure; engineering news—the use of robots in factories, new methods of transport and civil engineering projects; all aspects of ecology; the social implications of the new technology with special reference to human and medical advances, and research into areas concerning biomas and biotechnology, nuclear physics, marine biology and major scientific theories such as continental drift, alignment of planets, planitoids and astronomy. Above all, the articles attempt to put a human face on the world of science and technology.

The other weekly series is called 'Alternatives' and considers, as the name suggests, different ways, often controversial, of solving the major problems faced by society, be it employment, environmental issues or the Third World. The main contributor is Harford Thomas, supplemented by others with relevant specialist backgrounds. Topics covered have included the *Brandt Report*, the world's first comprehensive vegetable gene bank at Oxfam's department at the National Vegetable Research Station at Wellesbourne, community enterprises and studies of economic growth in various societies.

The Guardian is also especially rich in special reports and the like—always in-depth and erudite but readable and of great value in General Studies. Articles such as the three part series on 'The see-through society', dealing with computers and information systems and the privacy of the individual; a lengthy study of alternative fuels; a four-page report on word processing and an 'Economics extra' on an alternative agenda for party politics involving social change and new life patterns for what is termed a post-industrial society; job sharing, reviving rural life, 'villagizing' cities and the breaking up of big business.

In terms of the library encouraging students to broaden their knowledge in relation to general studies by watching and listening to documentaries on the television and radio, both *The Sunday Times* and *The Observer* provide a synopsis of the more worthwhile programmes appearing in the week ahead. These can be cut out and displayed, and made into a regular feature in the library. Taken a stage further, the librarian, being aware of the needs of individual students, can contact those concerned.

Periodicals

Many of the free and low-cost periodicals mentioned throughout this book (and listed in the Appendix) will prove of value in general studies. Some, however, are worth highlighting. Heading the list are the Council for Education in World Citizenship (CEWC) *Broadsheets*, which provide a succinct and readable account of current issues. Subjects that have been dealt with include the *Brandt Report*, the United Nations (disarmament and peace initiations), the European Economic Community, Japan's economy, the Horn of Africa, South Africa, Palestine, human rights, Israel and Iran.

Developments within the Common Market can be studied from the Commission's own journals *European Community* and *Euroforum*, consolidated in the one edition *Europe '82* (from January of that year), and *Forum Council of Europe*. There are also the *Europe Information External Relations* periodicals which numbered 20 by the end of 1980, dealing with a different country or part of the world.

Defence policies, arms capability, statistics and possible war strategies can be gleaned from *NATO Review*.

For a synopsis of economic affairs the monthly government *Economic Progress Report* and the *Bank Reviews* can be consulted, while for details of the unemployment situation, the *Employment News* holds the key.

The Third World and Britain's involvement in it is well covered in the Overseas Development Administration monthly *Development News*. Particular problem areas are often highlighted in *The World's Children*, a publication from the Save the Children charity. Specific countries where recent information from this source has proved invaluable have been Uganda (Karamoja), Bangladesh and Zimbabwe.

The problems of racial equality are always to the fore and these are well conveyed in the Commission for Racial Equality's *New Equals*. News concerning the coloured community, recent court cases, statistics, legislation and the new reports of the Commission are dealt with thoroughly.

Factors concerning energy are outlined in *Atom*, the *Esso magazine* and *John Deere News*. Topics such as solar energy, pollution, wave technology and conservation, as well as development in the conventional energy field are all included, while specific information on environmental issues is dealt with in the *Newsletter* of the National Association of Environmental Education.

The Association for the conservation of Energy, an organization composed of major companies, also publish a *Newsletter*. This looks into political implications of energy conservation, pricing policies and specific projects carried out by member companies.

News from within the two principal communist countries, Russia and China, is conveyed in their own sponsored journals called, respectively, *Soviet Weekly* and *China Reconstructs*. Both provide an interesting sidelight on their own affairs which can be used for comparative purposes alongside western sources of information.

Source books

Many of the organizations providing useful material for general studies are listed in the following source books available free or at low cost. A certain amount of duplication occurs in certain areas, which is inevitable when dealing with organizations whose functions can be seen as useful in more than one sphere.

The Department of Education and Science publishes the free *Inter-*

national Understanding: sources of information on organizations 1979—a handbook for schools and colleges. This publication of 158 pages is particularly useful in the following fields: child welfare, arms control and disarmament, economics, human rights, health, peace initiatives, politics and race relations. All the organizations prefixed by a code together with their addresses and services are listed alphabetically, followed by two indexes, one dealing with particular types of resources, the other the subjects covered. It is thus an easy matter to ascertain what is available for a particular topic.

The Department of Education and Science is also responsible for *Sources of Information on International Organizations.* Again, the publication is free and well indexed. The Commonwealth, European and other countries as well as British organizations are individually categorized, together with resources available, many of which are itemized with their titles, followed by a description, including costs, if any. It concludes with a list of 200 useful addresses of British organizations which can help in relevant education matters.

Following on from these is another government publication called *Overseas Development and Aid: a guide to sources of information.* Thirty-three organizations have been selected and once again there is an accompanying comprehensive index. This is especially useful as there is an emphasis on free material, together with its possible uses. Further to this guide is another published by the Overseas Development Institute called *The Development Guide* which outlines the purposes and facilities of nearly 200 organizations. That so many organizations exist on this subject is a point of note itself. They can, of course, prove useful in specific cases.

Continuing on the Third World theme, the Centre for World Development Education has a guide entitled *Agency Sources and Resources in the UK* on development education listing the main addresses worth contacting for material. Comprehensive details of resources are given including type of material and costs, if any. The emphasis with this publication is on religion and allied charitable bodies operating overseas.

The last main sourcebook to be dealt with is that of the Council for Education in World Citizenship with its low-cost *World Studies Resource Guide.* The Council is an educational charity and notable as being UNESCO's agent for distributing material. The guide is perhaps the most comprehensive of them all with much thought having gone into its compilation. Apart from a detailed contents list there is a thematic index enabling the enquirer to pick out relevant sources for a particular topic, followed by an alphabetical listing of the organizations. Three key questions are asked of each organization: what, where and why? enabling one to judge for oneself the usefulness of it as a source. Other sections deal with information on political parties, projects undertaken throughout the world and lists of selected and recommended publications organized by subject area. Major topics invariably touch on Third World developments and problems.

For more details on Third World studies one could do no better than read the article that appeared in *Youth in Society* in September 1983.[1]

With the emphasis in general studies being on students finding out information for themselves, it is worth making a point of explaining the usefulness of the aforementioned sourcebooks, as well as other reference works such as *Whitaker's Almanac* to them so that they can pursue their own lines of enquiry. Currency and accuracy are often the most important considerations in terms of the information required and these, it can be said, are available for the cost of a letter. For example, the White Fish Authority can be contacted for details of Britain's declining fishing industry; the British Medical Association can be approached for their guidelines on euthanasia; while UNICEF could be contacted for a current report on the dire situation in Karamoja. These are just three examples taken from the same week where the primary source in each field was able to provide valuable material on current topics.

REFERENCE

1   Youth in Society. 'Development Education Resources, a selective listing of relevant agencies'publications, visual material, games and simulations'. No 82 September 1983. 22-23.

Geography

Geography has made increasing demands on school resources as material in quantity has been required for individual projects at both ends of the academic spectrum, in both Certificate of Secondary Education and 'A' level work. There has also been the problem of in-depth studies, in particular areas, requiring current information. Added to this has been the failure of the Examining Boards to recommend texts appropriate to the new syllabuses, if, in fact, any have existed. The school has, therefore, had to draw on all its resources in order to provide relevant material, and especially those available at low-cost.

Three primary areas can be identified for which low-cost material is available:

a. Commodities.

b. The British Isles, in all its aspects.

c. Other countries.

These divisions are based on practical considerations taking into account the way geography is taught. In general, apart from films and journals, which will be covered in depth, the demand is for printed resources in the form of leaflets and booklets, and sheet material, either posters or maps.

In view of the variety of subjects geography embraces, some of which are studied in their own right and found elsewhere in this book, some general comments are called for on the material included in this section.

It is important to provide as good an indication as possible of the whole range of material available in geography, and to this end the list of sourcebooks holds the key. These, it will be found, are more than adequate, and range from those of a general nature designed with the geography teacher in mind, to those of a more specific nature, and included to demonstrate the scope of information on topics peripheral to the subject which is obtainable. Specific areas of geography which are covered in depth elsewhere are agriculture, world development (Third World problems) and environmental issues and appear under the respective headings of rural, general and environmental studies.

As periodicals and films are two types of materials that can prove particularly invaluable in any general geography syllabus it is worth examining them before going into detail on specific topic areas.

Journals

There are a number of free or low-cost publications which can be of value in specific areas of geography. The largest area served is that of individual countries through such titles as *Scala* on West Germany, *Japan Pictorial, China Reconstructs* and *Soviet Weekly*. All contain useful current information usually not found anywhere else at the time. There is no one source giving details of those available and their publications can be sporadic, but as they are usually financed by the government of the country concerned, the best plan is to approach individual embassies for details.

The Common Market Information Centre publishes three free journals: *European Community, Eurostat News* and *Europe '82*, each of value in keeping abreast of current developments in the European Economic Community.

The Council for Education in World Citizenship is responsible for two very useful low-cost *Broadsheets*, published in a senior and junior edition, on world affairs, highlighting a particular problem of the moment by providing the basic facts on the subject which serve as an excellent basis for discussion. Subjects covered include the problems affecting such countries as Afghanistan, Iran, the Lebanon and Latin America. Other similar news on world affairs is conveyed in

Development News published by the Overseas Development Administration and *NATO Review* which deals with aspects of defence policy.

Aspects of economic geography can be gleaned from the various commercial *Bank Reviews*, published by Lloyds, Midland and National Westminster which have already been mentioned. The last also contains economic surveys of interest to the budding geographer who can use them as models for his own projects.

Covering environmental problems are the Council for Environmental Education's *Newsletter* sent free to all local authorities (it is important for the school to make sure it is on the mailing list) and the Nature Conservancy Council's monthly *Earth Science Conservation*, a small but useful journal dealing mainly with geological issues.

Other worthwhile free publications must include the *Esso Magazine*, *British Shipping News* and *Dairy Education News*, each dealing with topics of current concern in their own respective fields.

Films

There is no current bibliography listing all sources of free or cheap to hire films, the nearest being the *A Classified Guide to Sources of Educational Film Material* published by the Educational Foundation for Visual Aids and the National Committee for Audio-Visual Aids in Education in June, 1972. In it there are over 170 possible sources in the four principal areas of geography — general, physical, economic and regional, with a fairly equal distribution over each area. Many of the sources listed do not provide items free and their charges place them outside the ambit of this book. This publication, albeit out of date does, however, provide a general indication of sources with their addresses. Most of the free or low-cost films available are produced by the relevant agencies of a country's government or a multinational company. In the former case they can be regarded as providing a general introduction to a country—its landscape, economy, people and its major products. Most are in colour, well produced (having in a number of cases won major awards), fairly up to date or released in the last seven years, have an English commentary and are of a length that one, or at most, two, can be shown in a lesson. Most countries are represented but there are exceptions, even amongst those which might appear as obvious producers because of their wealth and experience in the medium such as the United States, and especially amongst the developing nations of Africa. However, some material can be found on all the continents, even if it does not represent a balanced picture of the life to be found there. Such material would be likely to come from the Eastern bloc countries and other communist states as well as South Africa.

In general the films are distributed by the nation's representative in

London—invariably its embassy, and for those which do not fall into this category it is of value to identify the three major distributors concerned.

Guild Sound and Vision (GSV), perhaps the largest of the sponsored film libraries, has numerous free films in its catalogue ranging from those on the British Isles, angled to the tourist point of view, to those on the Bahamas, Denmark, Hong Kong, Iceland, Ireland, Japan, Malaysia, Malta, Brazil, South Africa, Israel and Canada, although for Canada the Agent General for the country makes a much wider selection available through the London office.

With the exception of Poland, which issues its own comprehensive catalogue, a very extensive library of films on communist countries is available through Educational and Television Films Ltd. All the films bear a small hire charge and are produced under the auspices of the various governments concerned. Those represented include Bulgaria, Cuba, Czechoslovakia, East Germany, Korea, Laos, Hungary, Mongolia, Russia and Rumania. Many aspects of geography are covered in what can be regarded as well produced films.

Finally to the multinational corporations which are generally representative of the oil industry and include such names as Shell, BP, National, Abu Dhabi Petroleum Co, and Elf Aquitaine, each of which produces a free catalogue. Films can be selected to show the production of oil, the various refining processes and its transportation throughout the world.

Those governments whose films are distributed in London through their various representatives, each issue a free catalogue (a comprehensive list of which can be found in Appendix 4). The best examples include West Germany, Canada, Australia, India, Italy, Denmark, Pakistan, Finland, New Zealand and Greece. In order to appreciate the potential of this resource it is worth taking a closer look at some examples. First, Australia, which is well endowed with film material as not only does the Australian Information Service issue a substantial catalogue containing approximately 250 titles, but each of the Territories also do so through their Agent General in London. Taking as an example the *Western Australia Catalogue*, this adds another 50 titles to the list on such topics as agriculture, minerals and mining, railways, water supply, hinterlands and country towns. Specific films include *Wesfarmers—working for the man on the land*, glimpses of agricultural operations in the state; a detailed look at the Central Hinterland, showing the wheat belt, industry and town of Northam in *Central Hinterland*, mineral riches of the area are portrayed in *Iron in Western Australia*, while *Western Freightway* shows the biggest rail construction in the free world for 25 years.

Subject areas

The catalogue of India Documentary Films presents 350 titles on virtually every aspect of the country pertinent to the geographer—agriculture, farming, forestry, irrigation, cottage and major industries, handicrafts, specific places and areas, transport and communications. *Cashew Nut* shows the various methods in the cultivation of this crop, one of India's most important exports, *See Haryana* deals with the landscape and places of note in this state, *Weave Me Some Flowers* gives a glimpse of India's textile industry and *Magic of the Rails* shows the recent construction of the Dandakaranya railway.

Source books

The Geographer's Vademecum of Sources and Materials has recognized the availability of a wide range of low-cost resources and it must be to this publication that the librarian turns in order to assess the potential of this material. The aim has been, in the compiler's words, 'to include as much material as possible of a kind that meets the twin criteria of relevance and usefulness...much of it from organizations outside the field of educational publishing and supply as such'. The *Vademecum* is well planned, containing three main sections: the first is an index of approximately 130 possible topics with the names of possible resources, the second lists the addresses of sources and names the kinds of materials available from them in some detail including costs, if any, while the final section covers sources and materials on countries. It must be stated, however, that a large proportion of the material quoted here does bear a charge which places it outside the scope of this book. The only weakness of this publication is that it is not published annually, the present edition dating from 1978 and the one before that 1971. This can be remedied to some extent by using *Treasure Chest for Teachers*, where classified sections under such headings as conservation, farming and agriculture, food, geography, minerals and mining, and transport and communication can reveal recent changes in addresses and material.

Addresses of embassies, which are a reliable source of some of the best and most detailed information, can be found in *The London Diplomatic List*. The most appropriate individual and/or section to contact is listed, and this is useful as it can have a bearing on the amount and range of material sent. Such sections include those under the headings of economics, culture, tourism, commerce, information and education.

Coming closer to home, individual government departments can be located through *Whitaker's Almanac*, while those responsible for disseminating information in local government, national and private industry and development corporations can be found in the *Register of members of the Institute of Public Relations*.

The Commonwealth—a guide to material and information services available to schools and to the public, published by the Central Office of Information, is especially useful as it lists not only specific information sources on countries implicit in its title, but also other relevant organizations able to help in world geography.

Another sourcebook providing information in the same area as the aforementioned is *Overseas Development and Aid—a guide to sources of materials* again published by the government. Altogether 33 organizations are listed, together with a useful subject index.

Finally, there are two further free government publications, both available from the Department of Education and Science and of relevance to world geography at 'A' level. The first is *International Understanding: sources of information on organizations 1979—a handbook for schools and colleges.* This contains over 150 pages outlining the details of the services of over 200 organizations. There are also two excellent indexes enabling the researcher to locate specific types of resources, be they information packs, films, research facilities or the like, and individual subject area topics such as countries, fisheries, industry or employment. The other publication is *Sources of Information on International Organizations, 1974* which, as the date suggests, is not as up to date as the first but is nonetheless useful for identifying a wide range of material which might be relevant. This, too, is well indexed with a comprehensive list of addresses and a detailed classified contents list. It must be said, however, that both these publications are perhaps of most use in the context of General Studies.

Supplementing the information found within the above four free government publications are two independently produced sourcebooks. The first, *World Studies Resource Guide*, published in 1977 by the Council for Education in World Citizenship and updated annually through supplements, includes information on over 100 organizations, together with further useful publications. The second is the Centre for World Development Education's *A Guide to Agency Sources and Resources in the UK* which lists 37 organizations and the types of material they have available. It also contains a catalogue of its own excellent free and low-cost resources.

A range of free and low-cost information on the subject of Europe and the European Economic Community can be located by the use of three free publications. The 100-page *European Community Information Series—a guide to the literature and an indication of sources of information*, published by the headquarters library of the Department of the Environment, provides a basic compilation of available material and addresses useful for advanced level work in geography. *The European Community—a brief reading list* is mainly concerned with books outside the scope of this book. There are, however, all the same, a number of low-cost publications and free leaflets included. For a concise listing of those free publications available from the head office of the European Economic Community, *European Community Publications* provides the answer.

Examples of free material include *The European Community: Who? What? Why? How? Where does Britain fit in?* a six-page leaflet ideal for sixth forms and *Ten Years in Europe: Britain in the Community 1973-83*, an illustrated 24-page supplement reviewing the impact of British membership of the European Community.

Sources of information on environmental issues in geography are well catered for by three organizations, the Conservation Trust, the Town and Country Planning Association and the Council for Environmental Education, and details of their services are found in the Environmental Studies section. Similarly, agricultural topics are dealt with under Rural Studies.

Commodities

Commodities include all the basic foodstuffs such as beverages, cereals, meat, fruit, sugar, milk products, minerals, natural fibres (cotton and wool), metals, rubber and tobacco, and the Commonwealth Institute issues *Commodity Leaflets* on most of them. Each leaflet in its four pages provides an excellent grounding in the subject covering such aspects as production figures, sources, history, processes involved and uses. Despite the Commonwealth context, the information is related to the world as a whole and provides a balanced picture. As well as these leaflets, the Commonwealth Institute also offers an excellent free loan service of slides, artefacts, books and posters which can be obtained if more in-depth study is required. Not as comprehensive in the range of commodities covered, though more substantial, are the booklets published by the Food and Agricultural Organization of the United Nations in their 'Better farming' series.

Considering the importance of milk and milk products, it is worth referring to the Rural Studies section where the resources of the National Dairy Council are examined.

Most commodities are represented by an organization such as Lead Development Association, International Cocoa Organization or the Tea Council; these organizations distribute a wealth of material usually in the form of documents providing production figures, annual reports, international agreements, consumption capacity and the world economy in relation to the commodity in question.

The large companies dealing in commodities themselves like Tate and Lyle, Lyons Tetley, and Allinson Ltd also issue excellent free material in multiple copies. This is usually quite lavishly produced and aimed at educational projects. Good examples would include *Where Rubber Begins*, published by Dunlop, a 25-page illustrated account with suggestions of things for pupils to do, and the seven-page handout of Lyons Tetley on coffee supplemented with two colour booklets.

The British Isles

Subjects for which low-cost material is available include the economy, regions, agriculture and forestry, transport, sources of power, water, industry and the environment.

Initially it is worth mentioning that the *Sales List of Reference Documents*, issued by the Reference Division of the Central Office of Information, contains numerous relevant low-cost publications, notably *Fact Sheets on Britain, Fact Sheets on British Industry* and *Reference Pamphlets*. Prime subjects covered are population, principal industries, industrial areas and transport.

Looking at each subject area in turn, the economy is dealt with in the quarterly *Bank Reviews* of the major banks, while for specific statistical returns, individual government departments can be contacted. For example, the Department of Agriculture and Fisheries for Scotland can be contacted for census returns on sheep, potatoes, pigs and vegetables for individual areas—known as the *Summary for Districts* and *Land Area Usage Figures* for information on total tillage, woodlands, rough grazing and cattle.

County and city councils produce excellent free handbooks, maps and brochures of use in determining the various geographical and historical factors responsible for their location and growth, as well as industrial concerns and transport services.

The New Town Association can also be contacted for those places within its charge and free publications can be obtained such as *The New Town* and *Britains' New Towns: facts and figures* as well as numerous offprints.

Also for specific areas of the country the national park centres and tourist board offices can be contacted for a wide range of maps, colour brochures and factual information. As an example the British Tourist Authority publishes full colour booklets on major areas of the country, eg South West England, South Wales and East Anglia. These provide a useful synopsis of the areas in question—a stimulating introduction for the less interested pupils. The Association of British Ports have a free brochure in colour on the 19 ports in its care. Details are given of them with a map—are they container, roll on, roll off, or bulk handling?

From time to time *The Guardian, The Financial Times* and *The Times* have special reports on regions of the United Kingdom, all of which provide an excellent synopsis of their subject containing information on population, industries, communications and future plans affecting them.

The Association of Agriculture is an excellent source of materials with such publications as *Types of Farming in Britain*, at 75p, and information sheets on most of the counties of England produced in conjunction with the Agricultural Development and Advisory Section of the Ministry of Agriculture (ADAS) each priced at 5p, providing an excellent synopsis of the current situation. Further details concerning this organization are dealt with in the Rural Studies section.

Forestry in Britain is catered for at all levels by the Forestry Commission where excellent low-cost and free materials include detailed maps of every relevant area, *Forestry in Britain/Scotland/Wales, A Brief Guide to Britain's Trees, A Guide to Home Grown Timbers, Annual Forestry Facts and Figures* and *Conservation, Recreation Landscape Design objectives*. There is also a recently published *Teachers' Handbook* explaining how to use forestry within schools. It includes a bibliography, details of four films, suggestions for lessons and useful addresses.

The nationalized undertakings in the field of transport yield rich resources, especially useful for comparative purposes for those undertaking projects at advanced level. Such information includes current statistics and policy statements, maps and plans, from the various British Rail Regional Headquarters, the National Bus Company and the Port Authorities such as London, Liverpool and Hull. The British Road Federation can also supply its annual publication *Basic Road Statistics*, which is a succinct account of the current situation.

Sources of power, namely the coal, electricity, oil and gas industries, have extensive resources available which are all listed in their respective catalogues. Methods of production, annual statistics, locations, sites and policy are all included.

The Water Council and its regional counterparts, the various water authorities, produce excellent free material for schools (in multiple copies). The information in the form of posters, maps and leaflets depicts the cycle of water and the various processes it undergoes from source to tap.

Nationalized and commercial firms invariably provide handouts in the form of glossy brochures as well as printed sheets which have been specially prepared with educational projects in mind. The information includes details of the history of the company, the factors taken into consideration for the location of the factory(ies), processes carried out, production figures and markets.

Countries of the world

Before embarking on these resources found outside the field of educational publishing, mention must be made of the in-depth coverage of countries given by the quality press. Starting with the surveys published in *The Financial Times*, these are probably the most comprehensive of all, each often extending to 20 pages or more in length with its own contents list. The information, supplemented with graphs, tables and maps, covers basic statistics of the country, area, population, gross national product per capita income, trade—imports and exports (emphasizing that with the United Kingdom), currency, general aspects of the economy and individual industries highlighted under separate headings.

The Times Special Reports are more general than the surveys mentioned previously in that they do not go into such great detail. They include items on the country of interest to the tourist—for instance, highlighting individual places of interest such as cities or areas, and important figures in public life. Information on industries is not neglected, however, and even though they might not be as exhaustive as those of *The Financial Times*, they could perhaps be regarded as more readable for the sixth former.

Finally to *The Guardian Special Reports* which are usually not as comprehensive as the two sources mentioned as each may deal with only major aspects of the country, be it the economy, an industry or a particular area. What the articles may lack in facts and figures is compensated for by a highly readable text.

Undoubtedly, some of the best sources of all for free and low-cost material are the embassies and their equivalents. There is, unfortunately, no definitive list of those that issue material. *Treasure Chest for Teachers* lists 52, the *Vademecum* 34, while *The Commonwealth, a guide to material and information services available to schools and to the public,* gives 37 relevant addresses and those just within its sphere. Also the embassies concerned rarely publish a list of what they have available as material is constantly being updated, put into a new format and re-titled. The best plan, therefore, is to consult *The London Diplomatic List* and to write to the appropriate section of the country's representative on an ad hoc basis as and when information is required.

Invariably most embassies can provide leaflets containing information on the country, for example, *Hungary in Figures, Information—Federal Republic of Germany* and *Chile—summary of basic data.* These leaflets can highlight individual aspects of the country and may be part of a series as in the case of those covering West Germany, where they total 21 in all, covering such subjects as territory, population and the economy. States, and particular areas, often produce their own brochure as in the case of the United States, Canada and Australia. Certain countries, where tourism is the principal industry, invariably have little to offer except on this subject. This would include countries such as Morocco, Spain, Greece and Luxembourg.

The leaflets themselves are usually fully illustrated and often contain maps which can, in a number of instances, be separate publications in their own right. A good example are those available from the Dutch Embassy where they are of a scale which makes them far superior to any atlas.

Still on the theme of sheet material, posters depicting life in specific countries can be obtained usually from the tourist section of the embassy. The posters generally portray the scenic attractions, often notable geographic and architectural features, and indirectly landscape patterns, and can serve to stimulate pupil interest in other lands. Excellent examples include those from Finland, Greece, Pakistan and India.

Following on from the printed leaflet and sheet material, information may be presented in a more substantial form by way of booklets and, indeed, books. For example, *Austria—facts and figures*, runs to 232 pages and is illustrated in black-and-white and colour, with a text complemented with many maps, graphs, charts and statistical data. *Austria Documentation*, about half the length and from the same source, the Austrian Institute, is mainly concerned with the history and economic growth of the country. *Facts about Pakistan*, of about 100 pages has only black-and-white illustrations but includes copious detail on the country's history, industry, power and water resources, communications and trade. *All This is Hungary, This is South Africa* and *Japan Today* fall into the same pattern.

Further information on the countries of the Common Market and the role of the European Economic Community can be obtained from the organization's representative in London. Free publications include *Facts and Figures, Europe at a glance, Finding Out About the European Community—(a guide to further information sources)* and *The European Community in Maps*—a folder containing an excellent series of maps with geographic and economic information about the European Community. If more information is required, for instance on current statistics or legislation, it is possible to contact the nearest relevant Depository or designated European Documentation Centre library, either in a university or a polytechnic library. *The European Communities* (Information Series): *a guide to the literature and an indication of sources of information* by Lena Partington should be consulted for a detailed appraisal of these further sources.

Akin to these Documentation Centres based at educational institutions are various centres specializing in the dissemination of information about certain countries, such as American Studies material to be found at

Manchester Polytechnic, at the Central Polytechnic of London and the John Jadkyn Memorial Museum near Bath; the Centre for Oriental and African Studies at Dorset Institute of Higher Education; and the Centre for Latin American Studies at Liverpool University. They are able to help with specific problems and can often advise on the most appropriate teaching material. Encompassing these and other possible sources of a similar kind is the sourcebook already mentioned, *International Understanding: sources of information on international organisations 1979. A handbook for schools and colleges.*

History

The majority of low-cost services and materials for this subject are found locally where there has been considerable growth in organizations prepared to supply resources of educational value; and teachers have not been slow to take advantage of them. In fact it would be true to say that the historian is to the fore in using resources of all kinds, and adapting his teaching methods accordingly. Furthermore, the Historical Association, the relevant teaching association, has done much to further the use of local resources, being to the forefront in offering much practical and sound advice, proven initiatives and ideas, all backed up by its own published resources. In view of the importance of this Association, the history department will invariably have taken out a subscription to it, enabling the school to take full advantage of what it has to offer. With this in mind, it is well that the librarian is fully conversant with its services.

The Historical Association's prime aim is to advance the study of history at every level, to publish material on all aspects of history and to act as a pressure group in every area that history can be promoted. With over 10,000 members it is not surprising to find that it is very active at the level of local branches, of which there are 80, in promoting teaching groups, meetings, lectures, conferences, a considerable number of which are heavily involved in dealing with local resources and source material. Of prime importance is its journal *Teaching History*—'a forum for new developments in the field and the best of current practice for students and classroom teachers'. A casual glance at this journal will quickly reveal new developments in resource acquisition. The articles by Margaret Bryant (1970) and by L Bolwell and C Lines (1972), which are included in the bibliography, sum up the role local resources can play in the school.

Of major importance also are the Association's publications, the majority of which fall into the low-cost category if the discount, which operates for members, is taken into consideration. The titles are continually being updated in line with current thought and alterations in the syllabuses. Altogether there are six major forms of publication. Starting with the largest called the 'General series', there are over 60 titles to choose from, each consisting of short essays of general interest on a major historical theme. Titles here include *Causes of the French Revolution, Chartism* and *The Atlantic Slave Trade and Black Africa.*

The 'Teaching of history' series, as the title infers, is aimed at making the teacher's role more effective. *The Museum and the School, The Use of Film in History Teaching* and *Computers in Secondary School History Teaching* are just three examples.

Next there are two groups of publications both on a similar theme of providing clear and succinct accounts: 'Aids for teachers', and 'Help for students of history'. The first has such titles as *The Transport Revolution 1750-1830* and *The Causes of the American Civil War* as well as more abstruse titles like *Investiture Disputes in the Middle Ages.* The other series in pamphlet form consists of bibliographies and short but authoritative statements on how to undertake the study of certain historical records, for example, *British History Since 1760, Local Record Sources in Print and in Progress 1972-76* and *County Records.*

Another series is composed of seven 'Information/Discussion' leaflets, perhaps of greatest value at the History Department meeting. Titles include *The Place of History in Interdisciplinary Studies* and *Developing the History Syllabus.*

Finally there is the 'Appreciation in History' series, seven illustrated pamphlets which bring together the results of modern research on particular topics such as English towns, revolutions, political parties and early Factory Acts.

Altogether this is an impressive body of information and, combined with the local activities of the Association, the historian will be well versed in what resources are available. Indeed, as already stated, the History Department staff will invariably be found to be leaders in compiling their own resource material from artefacts, making photocopies of old documents, collecting slides of local places of historic value, probably taken by a keen member of the department, and writing guide books.

It therefore might be said that the librarian will have little to offer in such a specialist field. Nevertheless, useful work can be done in bringing together local organizations involved in some relevant field, perhaps of interest to the History Department, and more particularly to the librarian when information is required for projects undertaken as part of the Certificate of Secondary Education course.

First of all there is the Local Studies Collection of the public library, whose principal asset initially might be a published bibliography enabling the enquirer or the class concerned to see at a glance what is available on any particular topic be it a village, historic landmark or dignitary of the area. This is especially useful on a class basis when projects have to be chosen, as those topics with most references will obviously have the greatest potential. Also by examining the bibliography and noting references prior to visiting the Local Studies Library, much time can be saved once the group is there.

The County Record Office, which usually makes provision for pupil visits, will invariably look up documents on a particular topic, if required, and photocopy them for a nominal charge. These can then be retained in the school for future reference—especially useful for topics of perennial interest. The value of microfilming old documents and even out of print books of prime historical significance, when their cost could be prohibitive, is well worth considering. (In the author's school this was done in the early 1970s and has proved of immense value).

Details of the holdings and publications of the local museums should be obtained and the school placed on the mailing list for details of exhibitions and talks held there.

It is not uncommon these days for local authorities to employ their own Archaeological Officer, usually based within the Planning Department. Their annual reports are worth filing for reference, whilst current activity can be gleaned from the media. The local radio stations often produce programmes on any new finds, as well as on the history of the area in general, and these could perhaps be recorded if relevant.

County Archaeological Societies are to the fore in publishing written records of the past in the form of their annual transactions. Even if these prove too expensive to buy, they usually make available offprints at low-cost on selected topics which will be of more direct relevance to schools. These societies are the best sources of information about speakers of note in the area.

Most places of historic significance have guides, maps and plans published about them and these are either free or low-cost. The local authority can be approached for details of older properties, perhaps conservation areas within towns, or listed buildings. This information could be supplemented with that from the local branch of the Civic Trust who are becoming increasingly active in approaching and involving schools in their good work. For the major historical buildings and sites which come under the aegis of the Department of the Environment there are the Government publications, listed in *HMSO Sectional List 27*, and most, if not all, costing less than £1. Smaller properties, still of interest to the historian, may have been documented by the Regional Tourist Authority in their brochures and guides or even by the owners themselves. Then there are churches which are often chosen for project work. These, if architecturally of note, will have their own publications

87

which are worth getting.

Finally to sources of information which may not be so apparent, which lie outside the county and can shed light on some place in the locality. Specific examples would include information on canals from the British Waterways Board, the history of the local bus company from the National Bus Company, details of old aerodromes, a popular topic amongst the boys, from the Ministry of Defence (RAF) and information about a local harbour from the British Ports Authority.

Invariably, even if such organizations cannot provide information themselves, they will be able to put one in touch with someone who can—perhaps, as in the author's experience, an individual who has been making a special study of the topic in question.

This kind of material is often not listed or not catalogued even at the Local History Library, so each enquiry has to be pursued as the need arises. The point is that what at first may be a good idea for a project and then appears to suffer from lack of information, can often be turned into a practical proposition if some detective work is carried out.

Visual material

Reference has already been made to the publications of local museums and these can be supplemented by material from their national counterparts, especially postcards. The British Museum has material covering such subjects as coins and medals, Egyptian, Greek and Roman Antiquities, while the Natural History section has some excellent material on prehistoric life—a very popular topic for project work where illustrations are always at a premium.

The major types of visual material are, however, posters and wallcharts. Their range is not large, however, neither could it be said that sources are unlimited. However, some useful free items do exist and the following examples should serve to make one aware of their scope. The National Savings Committee has published a range of wallcharts over the years: *Roman Britain* depicts all the major roads and towns, all with their Latin and modern names; *The Victorians* is an attractive yet educational sheet portraying 16 famous people of the age as well as fac-similes of contemporary etchings, taken from newspapers, of important occasions such as the inauguration of the Metropolitan Line, and Florence Nightingale in the hospital at Scutari. These are supplemented with a concise introductory annotation to the age. Then there is *Fashion Through the Ages AD 950-1937* showing 29 illustrations of women's costume over the period.

In the case of a nationalized industry, the Post Office has *The Amazing Genius of Rowland Hill*, a pictorial account of the major accomplishments of this man. These include the development of the postage stamp and the technology required as well as the administrative machinery necessary to administer the system.

The contribution of private industry to this type of material is exemplified by Dairylea and Robinsons. The first has *The Story of Transport*, which provides a clear idea of how present-day transport came about, and demonstrates the trend that vehicles of the future may follow. Thirty individual annotated line drawings convey the message and these are categorized into land, sea, air and hovercraft modes of transport. Robinsons, on the other hand, have been responsible for 10 *Great Documents of British History*, facsimile reproductions taken from such important manuscripts as Domesday Book, Magna Carta, the Death Warrant of Charles I and the map of the Battle of Waterloo. On the reverse of each is a brief account of the original document.

Finally, reference must be made briefly to the full-size colour wallcharts published by *The Sunday Times*, which are excellent in every way, and do bear a charge. By collaborating with authoritative sources such as the British Museum, by producing extremely vivid, clear illustrations, and balancing them with sufficient annotation, the final article is of a high standard. *The Kings and Queens of England* and *Prehistoric Life* are only two examples from a range that is constantly being extended.

Films

The selection is not wide but those that are available offer interesting and worthwhile viewing.

Some countries have made films depicting their history. Although these countries do not necessarily appear in the syllabus and the films are often produced for the tourist, they should not be ignored or regarded as of little worth. Two typical examples are *Treasures of Ireland*, tracing the history of the country through its art and *The History of Malta*, when one is taken on tour of its historic buildings—castles, prehistoric burial grounds, underground temples and forts from Phoenician times to British domination.

Some countries do, however, produce more relevant films. There is the 'Canada at war' series with 13 titles on the history of the Second World War, with such titles as *Blitzkrieg*, *Days of Infamy* (the Pearl Harbor episode) and *Norman Summer* (D-Day). Although these focus on Canada's involvement in the war, they nevertheless reflect the general course of events and provide a vivid account of what happened. Original newsreel footage is used throughout.

The German Film Library also has titles on a similar theme. *Resistance*, for instance, deals with German resistance to Hitler over the period 1933-45, using documentary evidence in the form of photographs, pamphlets and newsreel shots. Other titles deal more generally with the 20th century: *Thirty Years Federal Republic of Germany from Weimar to Bonn* and *The Iron Curtain*, which concentrates on the effects of those countries having to live close to the Communist bloc.

The Austrian Institute can be contacted for its free films—original footage taken at the turn of this century, on the Austrian/Hungarian Empire including major incidents such as the shooting at Sarajevo and the First World War.

Shell has three excellent films for the History Department—*The Road* traces the evolution of the English highway from prehistoric times through ridgways, Roman and drove roads to Parliamentary and coaching roads and thence to motorways and spaghetti junctions; *The Village* examines its beginnings in Bronze Age settlements, continues with its growth and role in the Manorial system and into the present day, and *Water Highways* tells the history of canals and transport, starting with the Duke of Bridgewater and his masterpieces in the 18th century, and goes on to look at the men who engineered, built and worked them. Shell also has film on the history of motor racing and the development of the internal combustion engine.

Another excellent film on the theme of transport is that of *The History of Flight*, made by CONOCO and distributed by Guild Sound and Vision; this film, covering the whole period from ballooning to space travel, was made for the opening of the Air and Space Museum at the Washington Smithsonian Institution, and is therefore of very high quality.

In conclusion, there are some general titles from the Central Film Library such as *Caring for History*, on the preservation of old buildings, and *Ceremonies of the Tower*, outlining the six traditional ceremonies held there.

Home Economics

Home Economics, embracing all aspects of domestic science, nutrition and cooking, is essentially a practical subject. There is, nevertheless, in teaching it, a necessary element of theory, a good proportion of which can be supported by low-cost material. This includes material on appliances and fuels, consumer education and standards, freezing, health education (beauty, child care and sex education), cooking ingredients, nutrition and dietetics, recipes, safety in the home, serving and cleaning methods. A stock of these resources can be built up and filed away according to subject, in either the Home Economics room or the library. They can be used for reference purposes, not only to supplement text books for project work (and most of the popular topics are covered) but for general interest and browsing over when practical work has been completed. Such is the format and presentation of the information that most pupils will find the material interesting, especially as it relates to items they are familiar with at home, and on television. In fact the pupils will need little encouragement to send off for it themselves. They can be made aware of what is available by having relevant items pointed out to them in the magazines they and their mothers read, and instructed to keep their eyes open when out shopping. Altogether it will make them more aware of what the retail trade is all about, encourage them to think of alternative products, and, one hopes, get better value for money when they compare and contrast what is on offer. In a society geared to pressurizing the buyer and where new products and energy saving are to the fore, consumer education has never been so important.

It is worth mentioning, before identifying the principal sourcebooks on this subject, that perhaps the most profitable exercise in acquiring low-cost resources on an informal basis would be to attend one of the large exhibitions such as Hotelympia or the Daily Mail's Ideal Homes Exhibition when a considerable proportion of listed material is to hand.

Needless to say the potential of this material has been recognized by the Luncheon Voucher Catering Education Research Institute (LUCERI), who have sponsored a comprehensive sourcebook entitled *Sources of Teaching Aids and Facilities for Teachers of the Science and Technology of Catering, Home Economics and Related Subjects*. Altogether, information about 600 organizations of potential use has been gathered together, their names and addresses listed alphabetically, and the use of a coding system makes it possible to see at a glance what each has to offer on both specific topics and in specific media. In practice, however, the requirements of the secondary school teacher are dealt with in the two annual supplements of *Home Economics Journal: Teaching Aids, and A-V Teaching Aids*, even though only half as many organizations are included. Their usefulness is due to annotated entries in sections classified according to subject interest, each naming items available, their age, suitability and cost, if any. Addresses are, of course, updated annually. (The publishers of *Home Economics*, Forbes Publications Ltd, have a number of highly recommended texts themselves such as the *Essex Cookery Book*—a concise practical introduction to basic cookery at 95p, now in its 28th edition). For detailing available information in specific areas, certain independent organizations provide excellent lists of proven sources, despite being authoritative publishers in their own right. Such organizations include the British Nutrition Foundation with information sheets identifying free material from various organizations—National Dairy Council, Kraft Foods, Blue Band Bureau, as well as numerous items of its own, the Health Education Council's list on numerous relevant areas such as *Food Hygiene, Home Safety, Sexually Transmitted Infections*; the National Marriage Council's *Young People in Relation—a special list of recommended reading*; the National Children's Bureau's *Spotlight on Sources of Information About Children*, and the National Association for Maternal and Child Welfare.

Though dealing with commercial sources, and not necessarily low-cost ones, the services of the Design Council, sponsored by the Department of Industry which operates through the Design Centre in London, are worth noting. The *Design Centre Mail Order Book List*, published quarterly, brings together over 1,000 of the best publications on the field of design and especially those applicable to the home. Those that must be mentioned are published by the Design Centre itself and include *Setting up Home; One Room Living; Rooms for Living; Children About the Home* and the 'Planning series': *Bathrooms, Kitchens* and *Lighting*. The good work of this organization, reflected in its awards, highly coveted by manufacturers, is essential to any teaching programme where the quality of excellence is demanded.

Government publications

HMSO is an excellent source of invaluable low-cost texts, with those of relevance outlined in the leaflet entitled *Home and Family*. The areas for which primary information can be obtained are health, social welfare and food. Such publications as *Health Education in Schools, Health Services in Britain, Social Services in Britain, An ABC of Home Freezing, Safer Pregnancy and Childbirth, Contraception Explained, Home Preservation of Fruit and Vegetables* and *Manual of Nutrition* serve as examples.

HMSO also, through its free monthly *Economic Progress Reports*, often highlights information of value in the Home Economics field. For example, in the issue for January 1980 (No 117), there was an excellent summary of current household spending, an essential aspect of the curriculum on this subject.

The government, through the Information Division of the Department of Trade, is unequalled for its coverage of consumer affairs. These are highlighted in its free publication *Consumer News*, which is up to date in such related matters as legislation, safety, education advisory services and protection. Material often freely available from other sources is also listed. The Department of Trade itself publishes a series of pamphlets, available in multiple copies, on buying household items from shoes to cars with the points to watch if satisfaction is to be obtained.

Independent organizations

These are rather limited in number but they do cover the important areas of the subject, providing sound advice and information of an unbiased nature.

The British Nutrition Foundation and the Health Education Council have been mentioned as excellent sources of information but their own free publications on such topics as healthy eating, heart disease and additives in food are concise and readable. Also concerned with choice of food and cooking techniques are the British Dietetic Association and the Vegetable Protein Association, while catering for specific kinds of cooking are the British Diabetic Association and the Vegetarian Society of the United Kingdom, the latter with an excellent range of free and low-cost publications such as *Basic Recipes*, *Dayplan* (vegetarian menus and recipes nutritionally assessed) and *Taking the Plunge*, all of which are sufficient in themselves to meet the demands of this section of the Home Economics curriculum.

The Royal Society for the Prevention of Accidents and the British Safety Council publish numerous free and low-cost items on safety care in the home. The former has *Home Safe Home*, *The Secondary Home Safety Workbook* and *Suggestions for Teaching Home Safety* while the latter includes *Clean up now*, *Good Housekeeping—it's not a dirty word* and *Housekeeping Check List* amongst its useful list of publications. These can be supplemented with information from the British Standards Institution, another body directly concerned with safety, especially in electrical goods.

Care of the teeth is a necessary element of Home Economics and this is adequately covered in the General Dental Council's low—cost material—posters, an excellent recipe book and a number of free booklets such as *Diet and Your Child's Teeth and Gums*.

In the area of child care, the National Association for Maternal and Child Welfare is able to provide a wealth of information on possible syllabuses which can be incorporated in the curriculum of Home Economics, especially for the less academic. To this can be added the *News Sheets* of the British Association for Early Childhood Education, each covering areas often chosen by pupils for topics such as *Stories and Story Telling*, *Young Children's Art* and *Talking to Your Baby*.

Food organizations: publications

Many basic foodstuffs such as flour, eggs, potatoes, meat, sugar and dairy products are represented by their own promotional organizations. Added to these are a number of certain branded goods which are also under the aegis of a promotional company named after the country of origin—cheeses from Switzerland, Danish agricultural produce and Dutch dairy products. Virtually all provide eye-catching yet informative posters, recipes and leaflets on their products and as each type of food is usually so basic to cooking, little imagination is required in using the material to advantage.

Industries: publications

Public utilities in the area of fuels provide a comprehensive range of resources sufficient in themselves to meet the demand in this area of the curriculum. The three fuels represented by the British Gas Corporation, the Electricity Council and the Solid Fuel Advisory Board can be researched, compared and contrasted to the fullest possible extent by using what must be the best available free resources in Home Economics. Each of the organizations provides a comprehensive catalogue. For example, the Electricity Council publishes *Understanding Electricity: films, film strips, posters, publications and wallcharts*, and there is a wide range of resources to choose from. Not all the information is necessarily relevant but that which is includes such films as *Kitchen Plan, Using Refrigerators* and *Living with Electricity*, 14 information sheets on such topics as cooking, food freezers and washing machines, and publications such as *My First Cookbook* and *Happy Homemaking*— 16 and 40-page booklets respectively, as well as speakers willing to give practical demonstrations.

Private companies also have a wealth of promotional material of all types available especially in the field of cooking ingredients, but as educational material it varies widely; it is important that information should be impartial and avoid too marked a tendency to advertise. On the other hand there is usually more than one firm dealing in the same product so it is possible to get information from a number of sources to be used for actual comparison purposes. Again, some products such as salt or cheese are so basic to the diet that their use as a theme, for instance in a recipe book produced by the manufacturer concerned, can hardly be said to be unethical when used in a classroom situation.

While the information available is generally in the form of leaflets and display material, the range of more substantial literature cannot be discounted. *A Guide to Nutrition* by the Energen Food Company is a free 70-page book containing vital facts on the subject, some of it reproduced from *The Composition of Foods*, published by HMSO. *Saxability—your household hints and cookery:* information published by RHM Foods, contains 12 sections, each covering an important area of cookery and home care, including first aid—the presentation is excellent with bold print backed up with colour illustrations. *The Persil A-Z of Washable Fabrics and Finishes* by Lever Bros, which has only a short reference to the branded product on the first page, is a veritable goldmine of information on all aspects of the subject, including an A-Z dictionary on fabric types and approved washing and cleaning instructions. These examples highlight the quality of the material available free from the nationalized industries and independent industrial organizations.

Wallcharts

This material is always of use in the Home Economics laboratory, combining instruction with an attractive display. Four principal areas can be identified, for which examples can be obtained: dietetics, types of food, washing principles and household finance.

In the first category, good examples are *Sensible Slimming*, containing information in the form of a calorie chart of popular foods produced by Slimcea Health Education and a vitamin C wallchart from Ribena. Unfortunately, one has to accept overt advertising implicit in these items as branded names are prominent in most cases, but useful information is nevertheless conveyed—at no cost to the school.

Types of food include foreign and British products with perhaps more examples from the former. Marketing organizations tend to be publishers and not individual firms, so undue stress on advertising is not a problem. One of the most useful organizations is the British Meat Promotional Executive with a series of charts at low-cost on cuts of meat.

Denmark, France and Germany all have a wide range of free posters available from their respective tourist offices highlighting their country's eating habits. Each is in full colour, and presents the information in an interesting and educationally useful way.

Procter and Gamble and Lever Products between them have material that shows the science of how a detergent works, the principles of washing efficiently and the international textile code of labelling.

The Bank Education Service has the widest range of material suitable for explaining to pupils the intricate world of finance in relation to household finance. While the charts are instructive, they are, unfortunately, not presented in as lively a fashion as to counteract most pupils' lack of interest in this subject, which is hard to teach at the best of times. They do, nevertheless, spell out vital facts on personal money management.

Films

In general, the range of films, despite a considerable number being listed, have limited potential in the classroom. The reason is that they either depict something that can be demonstrated better by the teacher, or that they can be regarded as nothing more than advertisements for the sponsors of the film.

Some films of use are those concerning sex education and, while these may bear a charge, copies may have been bought by the authority and retained in the local teachers' centre.

Modern Languages: French and German

With the introduction of many teaching courses allied to specific resource packages there is little need for other material which does not directly tie in with the particular course of study being pursued. That said, however, materials of a general nature, especially posters and wallcharts which illustrate the life of France and Germany are always welcome in the language laboratory, and films, if available, on the same general level, can always prove of interest and are worthy to be shown from time to time.

The following sources of information are confined to this country but in the author's experience the enterprising language teacher who usually visits the continent annually often makes a point of returning home with excellent posters and charts obtained gratis from government departments, tourist boards and town councils.

German

This subject is fortunate in having at its disposal the German Film Library, perhaps the largest single source of free films there is. Over 400 titles are listed in its catalogue and cover such areas as travel, sport, arts and crafts, history and industry. All in all they provide a complete picture of life in the country. Most are in colour, are well produced, although some are becoming a little dated, and to a considerable extent are available in both English and German versions. There is even a selection of full length feature films taken from German television—for these a small handling charge is payable.

The catalogue is in the form of a clip-binder making it easy to amend the contents as new titles are added or old ones withdrawn. Taking one relevant subject area, travel, there are 34 titles from which to choose; *Off-beat Germany* (1970), runs for 15 minutes, is in colour and deals with unusual tourist attractions. *Bavaria—impressions of Germany's South* (1975), runs for 30 minutes, is in colour, with English and German commentary, and covers the customs, art, architecture, agriculture and industry of Bavaria as well as providing a look at the state capital, Munich. *5 x Bonn* (1978), again of 30 minutes' duration, with a choice of commentaries, deals with five different aspects of the city— its inhabitants, history, its role as the capital of the Federal Republic, tourism and students.

The contents of the German Film Library are complemented by the German Institute in London and by the Goethe Institute in Manchester for the north of England. Both these organizations hold a wide range of other audiovisual materials which include slides, videotapes, records and cassettes on German literature, music and specific German language courses. The catalogue, although extensive, is free and is a valuable source of information.

Turning now to posters and wallcharts, the German Embassy makes freely available some excellent maps of the country and its regions—*The Rhine, Camping Areas* and *Weserbergland from Kassel to Mendin.*

The food and wine of Germany are well publicized by posters, available respectively from the German Food Centre and the German Wine Development Board. In virtually every case the information is depicted on colourfully annotated maps.

Finally, there is a government-sponsored monthly journal called *Scala*, available free, in both English and German editions. The contents cover a variety of topics with something that should interest everyone— current news, sport, fashion, popular music, politics, engineering, natural history, as well as information about great German figures from the past. The articles are relatively short and well illustrated with excellent colour photographs.

French

While there is a wide range of films (over 800 titles) about France from the Service du Cinema, a department of the French Institute, charges prevailing place them outside the scope of this book. The Service de Documentation Pédagogique of the Institute, like its German equivalent, also makes available a wide variety of other audiovisual aids. A few free films depicting the French railway system can be obtained from the Transport and Travel Film Library in London, but, in the author's experience, they are produced in such an avant-garde manner that they are unsuitable for general viewing. A useful range of posters/wallcharts is available free from three major sources—the French Government Tourist Office, the Food from France Organization and SNCF House, the last named providing material about the French railways.

Physical Education

Although this subject is essentially practical in nature there is nevertheless a small but useful range of low-cost resources which are worth consideration.

It is worth emphasizing at the start that the Physical Education Association of Great Britain and Northern Ireland is the main organization in the field and has much to offer its members. It is very likely that, in any secondary school, the Physical Education Department, or a member of it, subscribes to this Association, enabling the library, with, of course, the Department's co-operation, to take full advantage of the facilities available, which would be in the interests of all concerned.

At the heart of these facilities is the library containing over 8,000 books, documents and pamphlets, and over 460 periodicals, all of which can be borrowed by post. Supplementing this material are photocopies, translations, photographs and bibliographies. Up to date, specific information, which invariably is not available elsewhere, can therefore be obtained quickly at low-cost. In addition, for a more general current view of the physical education scene, there is the bi-monthly journal of the Association, *Action*. In this, within its showcase section, one is able to find out about all that is new in the way of free, or low-cost material, be it leaflets, posters or films; undoubtedly this is the most comprehensive listing of its type for this subject.

Another national body of great importance is the Sports Council, whose activities and resources are of special significance if the school is also a further education centre or community establishment. However, at a more general level, the free information of the Sports Council itself and its activities is of potential interest to all keen sports devotees. The free literature, all well illustrated, includes the *Annual Reports, Sport for All*—a general policy statement, *Hints on Forming Local/District Sports Councils, The National Sailing Centre, The National Centre for Mountain Activity* and the *European Sports for All Charter*. As a development on the above, it is possible for a small subscription to receive current news on what is termed activity leisure. This is done through the medium of the quarterly journal, *Sports and Recreation*, which incorporates the *Sports Development Bulletin*. The information includes full details of courses and coaching holidays at the National Sports Centres as well as courses, demonstrations and displays arranged in members' own areas.

Take Part in Sport contains a list of all the major sports encountered in this country, 54 in total, together with their relevant organizing bodies and associations' addresses, and courses, both national and local.

The booklets of the Sports Council are many and varied, ranging from technical reports through guides on the better use of facilities, to availability of grants. As a good proportion are written with particular reference to the various regions, their relevance can make them all the more significant. Many are low-cost or free. Of particular note to community schools are *Capital Grants and Loans for Sports Facilities Provided by Local Voluntary Organizations; Recreational Facilities; Some Ideas on Reducing Deficits; A New Approach on the Dimensions and Use of Sports Halls;* and *Rationalizing Sports Policies: sport in its social context.*

In the case of specific pursuits, the various organizations and associations are usually able to offer their own excellent low-cost publications or, at worst, provide booklets which contain current recommended titles, a proportion of which are invariably low-cost.

The Rugby Union and the Lawn Tennis Association are two good examples of organizations providing a wide range of invaluable literature, from the basic rules of the game through booklets on coaching hints to the more advanced skills required. Such titles include *Rules of Tennis; Tennis Practice and Exercise* and *Why You Lose at Tennis.*

Some eye-catching posters are also available which have undoubted worth in this subject, demonstrating basic moves and strokes, for example, those of the Amateur Swimming Association head the list, being colourful and informative with the minimum of annotation. The forms of swimming covered include the crawl, the breast stroke, back stroke, and the essential life-saving skills.

Sponsorship of posters by commercial organizations is evident but sporadic and a close watch on the media is necessary to find out what is currently available. Three excellent recent examples have been Taylor Woodrow with its involvement in building the new stadium at Twickenham, when it produced a poster outlining the positions of players on the rugby pitch; the British Eggs Authority with its *Laws of the Game—field and track*, and Philishave with three posters on the skills of football.

Finally to free films, of which there is an excellent range available, covering most of the sports taught in schools as well as those minority sports often adopted as options where the facilities exist. Starting with the basic curriculum found in most schools, the West German Film Library has the widest range to choose from. *Training and Records* is a series which shows examples from the Olympics in Munich combined with basic training technique explained with slow motion shots. All aspects of athletics, including football, rowing, gymnastics, throwing events and running are covered in 13 separate titles, each 10 minutes long. Football is also covered in greater depth in *King Football*, a series of 10, 10-minute separate films, each taking a major theme of the game such as tackling, heading and kicking. The films star top German players and excerpts are included from international matches to serve as examples. Physical education, gymnastics and dancing are not neglected and these are included in such titles as *Anatomy of Movement, Floor Gymnastics* and *Sport in Herbst.* These teaching and instructional films can be supplemented by more general material calculated to stimulate those pupils not particularly interested in sport. *Europe's Hour of Glory,* highlighting the 1974 World Championships, *World Cup 1974* and *100 Years of Football,* are good, well produced examples.

Another good source for a range of invaluable sports films is Canada House. *Your Move* encourages women to take up sport and shows that to be fit and active is not to be unfeminine. *I'll Go Again* is concerned with all the training required in order to compete in the Olympics, showing that even then success cannot always be assured. Besides these two noteworthy titles, there are others on badminton, cycling, rowing, climbing, canoeing. Canada House also has what is perhaps the best selection on winter sports—ice hockey, skating and skiing.

For specific sports not included in the above, a number of other sources can be contacted.

An excellent series of rugby films can be obtained from the New Zealand Film Library. *Giants of the Past* heads the list here, featuring matches involving the All Blacks, Lions, Springboks, Australians and the French teams. This is followed by seven other films, based on major international games. The fact that they are all in monochrome does little to detract from their usefulness.

Tennis can be observed from the point of view of the Wimbledon championships in a total of six films covering the years 1974-80. Each film, from Transworld International's Library, is approximately one hour long and features the main events with, of course, the finals in both the men's and women's championships.

A short but interesting film, which is available on video if required, on the history of racquet sports, lawn tennis, badminton, squash, called *Patterns of Play* is available from the Royal Mail Film Library. This was originally an Independent Television World of Sport programme.

Other films available of note are the *Prudential Trophy 1972 England v Australia* match from Guild Sound and Vision which also is the best source for films on golf; judo and other oriental sports titles can be obtained from the Japanese Information Centre, and *Safety in Mountains*, a must for all hill walkers is available from the Royal Airforce Film Library.

Religious Education

This subject has been extended in recent years to include not only formal teaching of *The Bible* but other religious and social issues, the aim being to awaken pupils' feelings about attitudes to broad moral issues in order that they can make up their own minds on religious matters. This idea of self-discovery has also led to the greater use of project material.

The library has, therefore, been called upon to supply a wider range of material than has hitherto been necessary. This material has also been of great value outside the religious education lesson as a source of material relating to themes in school assemblies and charitable ventures. It has also been possible for the library to display or provide for display purposes throughout the school a range of material reflecting the good work of charitable institutions operating around the world. Finally, the library should always have available to the more enquiring mind information on the world's many religions and faiths, especially in an age when the beliefs of individuals can result in decisions which affect society in general, while a knowledge of non-Christian religions in a multi-racial society is an undeniably desirable asset.

Looking first then at general sources, it is found that the majority of churches, including non-Christian faiths, such as the Baha'I, Hindu and Muslim faiths, provide free fact sheets which are sufficient for the enquirer to gain an insight into their beliefs and creeds. These can be supplemented by material produced by other organizations such as the Christian Education Movement (CEM) with its *Churches in Britain*, the National Christian Education Council's *Our Friends* series, or the British Council of Churches *World Religions in Britain*. Various specialized periodicals are also available, free of charge. These include *Anticipation*, published by Church and Society, focusing on scientific issues affecting religious thought; *Contact*, concerned with Christian communities' involvement in health; *Church Alert*, an ecumenical review of Christian social thought and action; the *Monthly Letter About Evangelism*; the Committee of the Churches' *International Affairs Newsletter*, dealing with world issues and possible peace initiatives, and the World Council of Churches' *Youth Newsletter*.

Likewise, the national charities have much material freely available including journals and posters. The journals vary in size and quality from the Royal National Lifeboat Institution's *Lifeboat*, the Church of England Childrens Society's *Gateway Magazine*, and Save the Children's *The World's Children* to the less substantial *Bother* and *Christian Aid News* of Oxfam and *British Amnesty* of Amnesty International.

Special mention must be made of Oxfam and Christian Aid, two of the major charities operating in a field of increasing concern, that of starvation and poverty worldwide.

Oxfam

Free 'Information sheets' covering 19 topics are available on all aspects of third world problems, ranging from specific details, including statistics on relevant countries, through to actual projects undertaken by the charity, and the better use of resources on a world scale. Each sheet is written with pupils of average ability in mind. Specific titles include *Poor World Series*, containing information on water, agriculture and child nutrition, and *General Development Sheets*, covering statistics relating to developing countries, unemployment, literacy and education and the world's refugees. While these fact sheets constitute the only free material, much more can be obtained at low-cost. Of particular note are the reports detailing accounts of Oxfam's work in specific areas; sixth form discussion papers on political and government attitudes to the world's poor; action packs concerned with intermediate technology; resource wallets detailing actual problems in certain countries; pictorial discussion sheets on world resources and topic booklets. All these resources are to be found listed in the free 40-page catalogue of Oxfam — *Education and Youth Materials 80/81—materials on development, change and the Third World for students and teachers.*

Christian Aid

Like Oxfam, Christian Aid has a wide range of free material covering world problems, although in this case it does have a religious slant which is not surprising as Christian Aid is an offshoot of the British Council of Churches. There is also a similar amount of low-cost resources such as simulation games, information packs and posters. It is worth mentioning the list of other sources of information at the rear of its catalogue and noting four organizations: Feed the minds (FTM), Save the Children Fund, UNICEF and War on Want, all of which are active in a similar field with free and low-cost items.

Turning now to those religious organizations which are of value in supplying material, the British Council of Churches (BCC) provides an excellent booklet called *Guide to Project Work in Religious Studies* which is of undoubted use in locating those organizations which have the most to offer. This outlines the major sources providing information such as addresses, recommended publications and costs, if any.

Starting with the British Council of Churches itself, there is a range of booklets available of particular value to the sixth form on controversial subjects. These can provide a background for discussion and include *Investment in South Africa, The Consumer Goods Society, Work or What, Some Reflections on the Arab Israel Conflicts* and *Rhodesia Now: the liberation of Zimbabwe.* (The World Council of Churches, the parent organization of the British Council of Churches, in Switzerland, can prove if help despite the fact that its free 80-page catalogue in four languages contains few publications at low-cost, as information in itself is free, and this is worth getting as background information on this major international institution may well come in useful.)

The Christian Education Movement (CEM) is of great help in the school as one of its principal aims is to 'work for the improvement of religious education' and to service the interests of teacher members of the movements especially those engaged on religious education. Membership is not cheap, but is well worth consideration as it entitles the school to discounts on publications, free specialist papers in teaching religious education and two free journals. Even if the school is not a member of the movement there is much low-cost material, much of which is heavily subsidized. The publications range from material of help to teachers in planning lessons to material useful in class, and discussion guidelines which have been put forward in recent years for the curriculum. Useful publications include *Planning an RE Programme, Birds Eye View of RE* which suggests aims for religious education for 5-18 year-olds, *New Approaches to the Assembly*, and the *Management of RE in the Secondary School*, 'Topic folders' on aspects of religion and having a social conscience, *Probes* for fifth-sixth formers, booklets on social problems, the 'Roundabout' series for remedial pupils and *Look* books for average ability 10-14 year-olds on leading a balanced social life.

In a similar vein to the above is the material produced by the National Christian Education Movement. Again there is a wide range of graded publications for pupils of all abilities, covering such topics as *Bible* interpretation, social problems, sex education, lesson planning and worship. Those of note include the *Green Book* featuring the Christian attributes of well-known personalities like Jimmy Saville, *Sex and Young Lovers*, the 'Search for meaning' series and *School Assemblies for the Eight to Thirteen Year Olds*.

The work of the Church overseas is covered in the material produced by the United Society for the Propagation of the Gospel (USPG) and the Church Missionary Society (CMS). The first has a free *Resources Folder* on what it has available, but this does not itself contain any worthwhile teaching material. Free and low-cost items can be obtained, however, and are especially useful on the affairs, often controversial, of African countries. Of value to any dedicated church group within the school are the *Window on the World* and *Parish Picture Service*, both of which are free services offered by the Society consisting of films, unmounted photographs and posters on social and church matters at home and overseas respectively. The Society also provides three low-cost periodicals dealing with missionary work and prayer: *Network Adventure; Thinking Mission* and *Quip*—all of more value to those with special interests in the church's work abroad.

The Church Missionary Society offers similar services, with a wealth of free material on its work. Again, as with the United Society for the Propagation of the Gospel, the material is of a rather specific nature and most suitable for use by any dedicated Christian group which is active in the school.

Rural Studies

This subject is well catered for by low-cost resources, the majority of which have been documented in two excellent sourcebooks. The first and more useful, as it is current and selective, is the Association of

Agriculture's *Bibliography of Sources for the Use of Teachers and Teachers in Training—agricultural material suitable for use in schools.* The other book, as it was published in 1966, obviously has many drawbacks, but its identification in detail of virtually all possible useful sources, especially government departments and agencies as well as associations which were in existence at the time, can provide an excellent indication of what may be obtained if not in terms of actual material at least in terms of sources, as many of these are still valid.[1]

The publications of the Association of Agriculture itself provide a good introduction to the subject with such titles as *Farm Studies in Schools; Farms and Schools; Farm Visits* and *The Chapman's Hill School Farm Experiment*. The books are written by experienced practitioners in these areas and have much to offer the teacher wishing to broaden his curriculum in rural studies, offering ideas as well as invaluable advice on all aspects of the subject. For information on types of farms, the Association's Farm Study Scheme, which comprises source material in folder format on nine actual farms, each one a model of its type, ranging from the small family farm in Kent to the hill sheep farm of the Western Highlands of Scotland, is an excellent proposition.

This type of information is also available within one cover in *Types of Farming in Britain*, an illustrated handbook with colour maps. *Agriculture in the Counties* also appertains to types of farming and comprises written descriptions, compiled in fact, by the Agriculture Development and Advisory Service of the Ministry of Agriculture and Scottish Colleges of Agriculture, for each county of the British Isles. The accounts are comprehensive without being too detailed and are certainly within the grasp of the average pupil. Details of climate and weather, soil, physical features, markets, land use and transport are all included and placed in context, showing their effect on agriculture in the particular locality which results in certain farming patterns.

Information sheets on the principal farm products—cereals, beef products, vegetables and salad crops, poultry and eggs—and nine topics of controversial interest, such as hedgerow removal, pesticides, straw burning, animal wastes and fertilizers are also available from the Association.

Finally, there is the low-cost *Journal of the Association of Agriculture*, published twice a year, containing statistics and background information on topics of current interest on the farming front, and including reviews of new publications.

It is also worth stating that the Association operates an advisory service which can be contacted for information on recommended material or sources of the most useful information on any particular agricultural topic.

Now to the body of resources themselves, which are best discussed under five subject headings, each one representing a major topic area where information is often required:

a. The countryside.
b. Animals and husbandry.
c. Cultivation.
d. Machinery.
e. Farm products.

(a) The countryside

The role trees play in the landscape is covered in the Forestry Commission publications. These range from those which identify the species, *Know Your Broadleaves* and *Common Trees*, to those which explain the need for replanting, such as *Timber—your growing investment* and *Forestry Policy*. There is also a series of posters called 'British forestry' covering 12 species of common trees.

Aspects of conserving the landscape can be pursued through the material produced by the Countryside Commission with the National Parks and the National Trust. The National Parks Centres are publishers in their own right and, taking the Lake District National Park as a typical example, the publications range from those on actual locations within the park and nature trails to those on natural history and the countryside, covering such aspects as *Trees and Forestry*, *Hill Farming*, *Fishes and Their Habits* and *Place Names* to name but four out of a total of 16, each costing five pence.

Fauna and flora are popular topics for which there is an insatiable demand for material. The Council for Nature is able to provide material on predatory mammals, recording schemes, legislation that affects wildlife and posters on rare British plants and creatures, while for more detailed information on plants the Botanical Society of the British Isles can be contacted for a low-cost series of posters on rare flowers.

Nearer home, the school can, for a small charge, become a member of the relevant local Naturalist Trust which issue *Newsletters* and information leaflets on reserves and local habitats. Local speakers can also be contacted and invited.

Some useful free material can be obtained from Shell on wildlife and flowers, with such fine examples as *Britain in the Wild*, *Moths to the Flame* and *Flowers of the Field*, just three of a series of nine pull-out supplements, each with a full colour centre spread supplemented with a detailed written description. The Forestry Commission also is a useful source of low-cost information on wildlife conservation, animals and birds. In its 'Forest record' series are 18 relevant pamphlets on the subject, with such titles as *Hedgerows*, *Titmice in Woodlands* and

Mushrooms and Toadstools of Broadleaf Forests.
Finally, a series of postcards depicting the majority of British birds can be obtained from the British Museum.

(b) Animals and husbandry

This aspect of the subject includes information required for a knowledge of farm stock as well as those smaller creatures often kept within the confines of the school.

Looking first at free material, the large animal food manufacturers produce information booklets on the management of farm stock. For example, BOCM Silcock publishes a range of booklets covering virtually all farm animals with such titles as *Sheep Management, Management of Horses and Ponies, Sucklercare* and *Calf Rearing.* All provide a good introduction to the subject and are available in multiple copies. Pets are catered for in a similar way by the large pharmaceutical companies who also issue colourful posters. The RSPCA and similar animal welfare charities also have an interesting range of leaflets and posters especially useful for information on the smaller kind of pets such as gerbils, guinea pigs, goldfish, budgerigars and tortoises.

Some of the best, if not the most authoritative, material at low-cost on farm stock is available from the Ministry of Agriculture via HMSO, and the relevant publication for any particular animal kept by the school is well worth having. Such creatures as poultry, rabbits, ducks and geese, bees and pigs, are to the fore. Other authoritative material is available from the various societies which represent certain breeds of animals—the British Goat Society is a good example. From it a range of booklets each dealing with a particular aspect of the animal can be obtained: *Breeds of Goats, Goat Feeding, Wild Food for Goats, Goat Keeping* and *Life Story of a Goat.*

In respect of the judging of farm stock, then the National Federation of Young Farmers Clubs has some excellent material available. *Know Your Farm Stock* is perhaps the best publication in its field, containing information, diagrams and illustrations on the breed characteristics of most farm animals.

In conclusion, there are three practical guides—*An Incubator in the Classroom, An Aviary in School* and *An Aquarium in School,* issued by the National Association for Environmental Education, which are especially useful in providing practical hints and outlining the pitfalls of introducing such things amongst children.

(c) Cultivation

The major fertilizer companies publish booklets on their products and the best ways of making use of them. One such firm is Fisons with eight colourful booklets on major gardening topics such as flowers, shrubs, bulbs, vegetables and diseases. Taking as one example, *Growing Under Glass with Fisons*; this runs to 16 pages and covers aspects of greenhouses such as type of structure fundamental in cultivation, planning the seasons, details of pests and diseases and propagation and concludes with a month by month guide in tabular form for growing vegetables. The information is presented in a readable and concise way with headed paragraphs and numerous accompanying illustrations.

Charts and posters are also available with notable examples being *How to Control Pests and Diseases* from Murphy Chemical (which also includes a vegetable growing guide) and ICI/Carters Seeds month by month *Guide to Home Grown Vegetables.*

It is as well to mention at this stage the British Agrochemical Association whose free publications outline the need for scientific methods in crop protection. They include *Pesticides in Agriculture*, the submission of evidence to the Royal Commission on environmental pollution; *The Safety of New Pesticides in the Environment* and *Why Feed Pests?* Relevant details are given in a clear and concise manner backed up with statistics in graphs, charts and tables and references where necessary.

A recent publication is *The Fight for Food*, a 16-page glossy publication covering 12 major aspects of pesticides from their efficiency in agricultural terms through their scientific constituents to the law and their ethical future uses.

Shell Chemicals also produces a similar type of publication—*Chemicals on the Farm*, which also includes information on fertilizers. References and a further reading list is given as well as a useful guide to the major agrochemicals in common use.

Both these booklets are available in multiple copies.

In contrast to the use of chemicals in cultivation is that view put forward by the Soil Association whose ideas have generated much publicity in recent years. Again there is a useful range of material available describing and justifying their methods: *Garden Compost* and *Farming Organically* describe the basic ideas; *The Value of Weeds, Some Good Companions* and *Make Your Plants Work for You*, deal with the inherent characteristics of plants and how they can be used to the gardener's advantage while *Friend and Foe in the Garden* is concerned with the way nature herself is able to control pests.

(d) Machinery

Of great value here are the technical leaflets produced by the manufacturers on their range of farm equipment—tractors, combines, milking machines, balers and the like. They are available free on request

107

and can be filed according to subject providing a base for the Certificate of Secondary Education projects often chosen on these topics. This basic information can be supplemented by full colour wallcharts showing in greater detail specific parts of engines—for example David Brown's *Hydra Shift Semi-automatic Gearbox* and its *1412 Sectionalised Tractor*. This firm also supplies offprints of articles which have appeared in the national agricultural press: examples are *Power Steering, Disc Brakes* and *Assessing HP*.

Other useful publications can be obtained on the history of farming. Three of the best examples are *Perkin's History of Power in Agriculture*, a large colour chart showing the people, inventions and machinery that have transformed farming from the earliest times; Castrol's booklet *Ploughing Through the Ages*, and a Science Museum booklet *Agricultural Handtools to Mechanisation*.

Various films from the manufacturers can be obtained on their products. The outstanding sources are John Deere and International Harvester. Machinery is shown in a working context both at home and abroad. Indirectly, information is conveyed of different farming methods making them more valuable than they might at first appear.

(e) Agricultural products

Of all the products, milk, butter and cheese have the best range of low-cost resources available due to the excellent educational resources of the National Dairy Council (NDC). The best of the material is to be found in full colour wallcharts which cover such aspects as the step by step production of milk; *At the Dairy Farm* and *Milk for the Nation, The History of Milk, How Cream and Butter are Made* and *How English Cheese is Made*. Two others show the dairy areas of the United Kingdom and the different traditional English cheeses. This information can be supplemented with *Dairy Education*, the quarterly journal of the National Dairy Council. To take the summer edition, 1980, No 48, as an example of the kind of information conveyed, this includes details of a new booklet and film *The Milk Year*, a new Milk Marketing Board creamery at Severnside, the development of new dairy products and food labelling.

The British Wool Marketing Board produces some useful material on its products, ranging from a free general information leaflet to a low-cost, well illustrated book of British sheep breeds. Other items are a large wall map showing the distribution of sheep and manufacturing sources in the United Kingdom, two booklets *Wool in History* and *Growing Wool*, and wool samples of 12 different breeds of sheep.

Other agricultural products for which there is a useful range of material are cereals, potatoes, mushrooms, English fruit, egs and meat.

Subject areas

Some of this information is perhaps more applicable to the commodity section of Geography where it has been dealt with more fully.

REFERENCES

1 Wright, R T *Source Book for Agricultural Education.* Moray House College of Education, 1966. 132pp.

Science

The topic range of low cost resources available in this subject is not large considering that science in the comprehensive school includes chemistry, biology, physics and possibly aspects of design technology. The resources available however, do cover core areas of the subject and as they are produced by multinational firms, such as Shell, ICI, Unilever, and public utilities such as Electricity, Gas, Water and Atomic Energy authorities, which all have education departments, they are generally excellent in quality. All formats of resources are represented, often models of their kind, be they journals, wallcharts, films or simply information leaflets or booklets and, in some cases, they are free. There is also the added bonus in this subject area of having an organization geared to the dissemination of current information of value to teachers—the Schools Information Centre on the Chemical Industry, which brings together relevant information in its *Bulletin.*

Before discussing the resources which have proved their value in the school, reference must be made to the extensively researched publication, *Useful Addresses for Science Teachers,* which runs to over 500 pages in length, the most recent edition having been published in 1974. The main sections relevant to this book are those dealing with wallcharts, posters, films, sources of information from national organizations and societies, booklets and leaflets for pupils/teachers, all of which comprise about one fifth of the book, the rest dealing with apparatus and equipment, supplies, courses and the like. The usefulness of the book is somewhat impaired with short annotations for each entry—little detail is given of the type and relevance of resources available, thus making it hard for the reader to decide which organization will yield the most useful material. However, despite the book's shortcomings (and its date of publication must not be disregarded), it has proved of value in estimating the likely range of material available.

The other sourcebook is that published by the National Centre for School Technology, *Directory of Resource Material for Teachers of Technology in Schools, 1976*. Again, as with the former publication, current details are lacking, but the sources in general remain valid and, with much more information about individual items such as titles, costs, if any, age range, a good indication of what is on offer can be deduced. The topic headings of the 80 or so subjects listed which are worth considering include atomic energy, corrosion, plastics and man-made fibres.

Before examining those resources of direct relevance to the curriculum there are two organizations worthy of mention, whose work is of general interest to those operating in the field of science. They are the British Society for Social Responsibility in Science and the British Association for the Advancement of Science.

The first aims to make scientific and technical knowledge available to non-specialist workers and laymen. To these ends it publishes *Hazards Bulletin* and a journal called *Science for People*.

Coming now to resources of use in the classroom, two teacher-based organizations are worth noting—the Association of Science Education (ASE) and the School Natural Science Society, which both provide a wealth of low-cost material. The first has publications which include the 'Study' series, consisting of seven titles in all, dealing with the curriculum; titles include *Science in the Middle Years, Resource-based Learning in Science* and *Non-streamed Science: a teacher's guide*. There is also a range of publications—*Safety in the Laboratory*, an illustrated leaflet available in multiple copies for the instruction of pupils in basic safety procedures is perhaps the most useful. Complementing this is a range of 99 different chemical labels for marking containers, each incorporating a hazard warning and the first-aid procedure necessary in event of an emergency.

One resource worth mentioning at the outset which has received much acclaim from teachers in science is the series of films made by Phillips Petroleum called the *Search for Solutions*. This consists of nine 18-minute films 'designed to serve as an avenue of involvement and a way to build renewed interest in science and technology.' Twenty named prominent scientists were involved in the production and the illustrated teacher's guide runs to 150,000 words. The material can be adapted to suit different teaching disciplines, level of abilities and objectives which cover such pertinent topics as nuclear power, science in literature, medical research, the actual image science conveys to the ignorant and the social and political issues science can foster.

The other organization, together with its junior section, the British Association of Young Scientists, is the largest science-based group supported by students. Together they publish a variety of general interest material which includes *Spectrum* and *Bay News*, two journals containing information on current scientific issues. It must be emphasized that these groups do much in the way of organizing conferences, talks, lectures and the like in which pupils and staff can be involved and including the literature in the library can provide a greater awareness and impetus to scientific thought and deed.

The Association has been responsible for the *Lamp Project*, a modular science course for the less academically motivated pupils in the 14-16 year-old range. Fifteen topics are covered with publications for each unit comprising notes and activity sheets for the teachers, with experiment and information sheets for pupils. Topics include heating and lighting a home, flight and gardening. There are also general publications covering such aspects of science as chemical nomenclature, symbols and terminology and information for laboratory technicians.

Finally, the Association has had published, on its behalf by John Murray Ltd, 13 books regarded as primers in their respective fields. Examples of titles are *Plant Physiology, Catalysis* and *Light*.

The School Natural Science Society publishes nearly 50 booklets on those topics usually taught in most schools. Each has an author regarded as an expert in his field. The relevance and usefulness of this material can be judged by the fact that a number are suitable for Nuffield Secondary Science courses.

The Schools Information Centre on the Chemical Industry

In view of the importance of this organization in the field of science it is useful to examine in some detail what it has to offer. First, though, some information on the organization itself.

The Centre was established in 1970 with a grant from BP in order to disseminate information of interest to schools in those industries involved in chemical processes. Since that date, however, extra funding has been necessary, firstly from the Chemical Industries Association (CIA) together with Esso Chemicals and later from the Polytechnic of North London and the Department of Industry. Altogether some 3,000 schools are on its mailing list. The Centre publishes its quarterly *Bulletin* which is a veritable goldmine of information about new free resources available from industry, some of which are included in the mailing, saving the school the cost of postage. There are no charges whatever. Other information includes current news and opinion on such subjects as the curriculum, careers, school-industry liaison, industrial statistics and project ideas. The Centre also initiates and supports the production of materials on industrial topics which have direct relevance to teaching programmes and, perhaps most important of all, publishes information sheets on free or low-cost resources on particular topics. These are worth listing here as they cover some of the most important areas for which low cost material is available on particular topics. These topics include beer and wine making, colour, cosmetics and perfumes, paints and detergents. (A full list is included in Appendix 1). The information sheet on colour, for example, lists 11 free items, while the one on cosmetics and perfumes, always a popular topic with girls, but one on which it is not easy to find information, lists three items.

As a footnote to the mention of the Centre, it has published two excellent free publications on the co-operation now taking place between schools and industry. Firstly, there is the 20-page booklet *Firms: industry liaison—a guide to existing activities*, which gives brief details of some of the many organizations producing material and offering help to schools. Most of these organizations have, incidentally, been until recently confined to the chemical and allied industries, but they are now expanding outside this area. Details of curriculum development, national organizations involved in this field, general information sources, work experience and resource material from industry are all covered, together with an index and glossary.

The other publication is *Resource Directories of Local Industry—a guide to their compilation.* This shows how a successful one is produced for the Leicester area and this can serve as a model for anyone intending to compile one for another area. The process is described simply in step by step stages and there is also a large appendix containing facsimile forms of the type a school would need to send out to firms enquiring for details of possible resources and co-operation.

Journals

The principal journals, all of which are free, originate from one of two sources—the oil industry or the government.

Taking first those concerned with the oil world, there are Castrol Educational Division *News* and *Shell Education News*, both geared towards disseminating information on their own new resources and developments within their own organizations. The purpose of Castrol's education division has been defined thus: 'to promote interest in, and disseminate information about all aspects of motoring, motor engineering and advances in automotive technology, to provide resources for teachers at every level and to be the prime source of teaching aids on motor safety in Britain.' This has certainly proved to be the case, but the material is not cheap, and cannot be regarded as low cost. However, the free news bulletin, Castrol Educational Division *News*, provides information on new motoring technology and oil, sports news, and an interesting correspondence column where teachers can air their views and ideas.

Shell Education News on the whole takes a much wider view of oil resources as well as education trends and curricula. Details of all new teaching resources of the Shell Education Service are published in the journal and, in this case, are entirely free. In the summer edition of 1980 there is an excellent article, reinforced with statistics, on the small percentage of women graduates taking up careers in industry, details of new booklets from the Shell Briefing Service and information on developments in future fuels, biomas, detergency, oil fields in the North Sea, petrochemicals, projects undertaken in varius schools, nesting habits of birds, plastics and waterways. As a follow-up to these articles, four booklets and a fact sheet can be obtained free of charge, while two films may be borrowed without cost.

Esso also publishes its own magazine—a far more glossy and substantial affair than the two already mentioned, which contains fewer but in-depth articles. *Esso Magazine 115* (Autumn, 1980) contains five articles: two on aspects of the environment, with details about countryside shows and the Pembrokeshire footpath, one on weather forecasting, another on energy facts and the last one on North Sea Investment. There is no mention of follow-up material or teaching resources.

The three journals published by government departments are *Project*, *Industry/Education View* and *School Technology*. *Project* is concerned with engineering for young people at school and serves to stimulate their interests on the subject showing them the importance of the engineer in society. It is well produced, containing full colour illustrations, drawings, plans and maps, where appropriate, to supplement the text, often dealing with complex subjects, which are lucidly explained. Articles are written by experts in their field, with, for example, the Director of the National Computer Centre on microelectronics, the Midland Editor of *Motor* on safety glass in cars, or the Deputy Editor of *Power Use* on fusion power. A wide range of subjects is covered from the frontiers of science to the processes of everyday technology with, from time to time, biographies of famous engineers and inventors. *Industry/Education View* features news, views and other information likely to be of interest to those concerned in promoting schools-industry liaison. It aims to act as a link between the different organizations active in this field and to spread the ideas being developed in various parts of the country as widely as possible in the hope of stimulating others to take action in their own area. Many of the articles are therefore about what individual schools and education authorities have succeeded in doing in the world of engineering, technology and science. It deals, as well, with government reports and conferences, gives details on current competitions like the Young Engineer for Britain and Young Enterprise, but what perhaps may be of most interest to the library are the references to new resources from the various organizations and firms mentioned.

School Technology deals mainly with actual science-based projects that have been carried out in schools. Each is documented fully with all the data and is amply illustrated. Other subjects covered from time to time are curriculum design and current trends in teaching science in a design and technology context. The resources of the National Centre for Science and Technology, the publishers of *School Technology*, are fully documented in each issue.

Two free journals which fall outside the above areas are *Telecom* from British Telecom, dealing with current communication technology, especially important when requiring information on viewdata and the like, and *Atom*, the journal of the United Kingdom Atomic Energy Authority, the most authoritative publication on nuclear power.

Now to a consideration of the resources themselves as they are used in the classroom. As has already been stated, the majority of them are produced by comparatively few, albeit the largest organizations, so a closer look at them should give a good indication of their range. The writer makes no excuses for the fact that films are to the fore as these have been found to be the most in demand.

Starting with Shell which has a well-balanced range of material, some of which—*Shell Education News* and the booklets, produced by the Shell Briefing Service—has already been mentioned, one finds quality second to none and as no charges are imposed, it is essential for the school to be placed on the mailing list. Topic-wise, the subjects cover aspects of the composition of oil, detergents, types of oil, engines, chromatography, chemicals from oil, natural gas and environmental topics, allied to biology. Most publications are available in sets of up to 10 copies, are updated frequently, have accompanying diagrams and illustrations where extra clarification is required, are well laid out with contents lists and boldly printed paragraph headings and conclude with further references to 10 other free publications and films from rival firms. Examples are *Experiments in Detergency, Facts about Plastics* and *Energy from Biomas*. Most of the ecology-related material is in the form of annotated wall posters and charts with such titles as *Insects' Life Histories, Conserving Our Environment, Oiled Sea Birds, Wildlife on the Thames* and *Birds of the North Sea Passage*. These, together with the booklets, comprise a resource list that totals upwards of 40 items. The list of films is constantly being added to and updated—14 new ones in 1979, bringing the total to over 100. The body of information conveyed is large, though it must be said not all the films are to do with science.

One aspect of considerable importance is that many are being made available on video-cassette. Besides the coverage of oil itself from extraction to distribution, on which there are 17 films, other subjects include engineering principles, automotive engineering, the science of aviation and petrochemicals.

From Shell to BP, the other giant of industry with a wealth of education resources available, though in this case they are not entirely free, one finds available, at low-cost, an excellent range of wallcharts on motor car engineering and oil technology. Other publications include the 10 'Cavemen' booklets dealing with the properties, uses and manufacture of plastics and chemicals; *Science Teaching for ROSLA*, a handbook for teachers containing over 100 ideas for investigating with detailed studies in oil, plastics and paper; *Industrial Processes for Sixth Form Chemistry*, covering new ready-planned projects, each one containing industrial information about processes and market demand, together with practical instruction, and *Global Energy Resources*, a teacher's handbook on this important subject.

Still considering the oil companies, Esso Petroleum has a wide range of films on offer, again a good selection on aspects of oil and general science and technology, with such titles as *Change of State*, discussing the physical changes that occur when liquids are heated or cooled, or *Sixteen Pairs of Eyes*, dealing with computer control in a modern complex refinery. Of special note is a series of 33 films especially aimed at science teachers showing new ways by which familiar experiments can be demonstrated to pupils, bearing in mind the Nuffield Foundation courses. All the films feature practising teachers. Other films, all recently produced, on oil extraction and related industry, are available from E G Aquitaine and Abu Dhabi Petroleum Company.

From the oil giants we pass to the chemical multinationals whose names include, above all, ICI and Unilever.

ICI outlines its resources in a well laid out publication called *Schools Liaison Questions and Answers*. Altogether these represent most of the chemical and allied products generally encountered in the industrial world—fertilizers, catalysts, nylon, polyester and inorganic fibres, alkalis, acids, chlorine and fluorine derivatives, sodium, salt, dyes and pigments, rubber chemicals, bioacids and many other organic compounds such as paints, petrochemicals, pharmaceutical products, plastics and plant protection chemicals. All these are manufactured by ICI on various sites throughout the country and it is from the particular works or division that the free publications on their products must be sought, each works or division having a schools liaison officer.

The publications range in suitability for particular abilities of pupils, depending on the product. For example, *What is Paint?*, *A First Look at*

Plastics or *What Goes On in Chemical Plant* have a general suitability for most students, while *The Manufacture of Polymers* is more academic in content.

Available from ICI head office, however, is some reasonably priced literature which ranges from wallcharts such as a *Periodic Table of Elements,* together with multiple copies of the same for class use with junior forms, to some more advanced booklets on antibacterials, chemical engineering, pesticides, fertilizers and inorganic chemicals. Full details of the publications are given so the enquirer has no doubt as to the suitability of the material for any particular class of students. All the material is well produced with bold printing, written in the simplest style possible commensurate with technical jargon, and supplemented with diagrams. *Schools Liaison* itself contains a list of useful addresses which could prove of great value to sixth formers interested in obtaining information on particular aspects of careers in the science world.

Unilever makes available, all for a nominal charge, three separate series, each in class sets, of booklets aimed at different academic levels of students. The contents of these, as with all material available from this firm, are detailed in the *Unilever Educational Publications Catalogue.*

First there is the 'Ordinary' series of six booklets for pupils aged 13-16 years. Without resorting to obscure technical language and supplemented with illustrations, photographs and diagrams, these cover aspects of detergents, vegetable oils and fats, food preservation, margarine and cooking fats, toiletries. The salient points of the scientific basis behind these topics are explained simply, and made interesting by bringing together historical and current factors in everyday commodities and processes.

The 'Advanced' series for sixth formers, again produced with attention to detail, is amply illustrated and includes micrographs, making it very technical in nature. All the booklets provide a good basis for the application of the scientific elements involved, such as water, the chemistry of proteins and micronutrients.

'Laboratory Experiment' leaflets, constituting the final series, have been written for the science teacher and describe industrial-based experiments which can be carried out in the laboratory by pupils in the age range 15-18 years. Details are given in a clear and concise form with attention being paid to the necessary equipment required. Virtually all the experiments have relevance to most science courses pursued in schools. Four typical experiments included involve the preparation of soap; making an emulsion; the rusting of steel and the determination of the total hardness of water.

Though Unilever has an extensive film library, the hire charges imposed preclude them from inclusion in this book.

Another major source of material dealing with chemicals worth considering is Courtaulds, who make available a range of free films on their patented products such as Evlan, Rocel and Rayon, dealt with in the films *The Evlan Cover Story*, *Focus on Rocel* and *Rayon — first among fibres*. Basic principles of man-made fibre production, their properties and applications, are explained, which is very useful when information is required on those complex chemical processes involving cellulose chemistry. Three other films, *Family of Fibres; What's Afoot?* and *Carpets — the making*, can also be obtained when details of the processing of fibres into fashions and carpets are covered.

Finally Monsanto published *The Chemical Facts of Life*, a 'candid discussion of chemicals, their history, use and misuse, testing procedures, benefits and risks to mankind'. Though the subject is seen from various viewpoints, no specific contributions are mentioned. On the whole, however, the treatment is well balanced.

Next to be considered are the resources concerned with sources of power—electricity, nuclear power and gas. The United Kingdom Atomic Energy Authority and the British Nuclear Forum have a wide range of material which, at the one extreme, includes a free mobile 15-panel exhibition on nuclear power. Other more mundane resources are the journal, *Atom*, already mentioned, pamphlets such as *Nuclear Waste Disposal*, and *The Need for Nuclear Power*, wall posters on power stations, speakers and films. Those films also available on videocassette deal with the need for nuclear power—*Energy — the nuclear option* and *Energy in Perspective*—types of reactors—*The First Reactor* and *Nuclear Power Reactors*, and radioactivity and recycling—*Windscale — nuclear fuel recycling* and *Using Radioactivity*. Where possible they avoid jargon and intricate technicalities, aiming to interest the layman while, at the same time, making him fully conversant with the principles involved.

The resources in electricity are fully catalogued in *Understanding Electricity* published by the Electricity Council. They include information sheets, booklets (available in class sets), wallcharts, posters and films. All are free. In general the information lists and booklets deal with the rudiments of electricity and supplement the information conveyed in the films such as *How Electricity is Made and Transmitted* and *Transmission for Power*. The posters and wallcharts, however, stand out as self-contained resources, some of them being reprinted and produced from commercial sources such as *Pictorial Education Quarterly* and J Bartholomew and Son. They are all in colour, full size (1m × 620mm) and annotated clearly. From them details can be gleaned quickly on all aspects of electricity production, its distribution and uses in the factory and home.

There is also a 'Famous scientists' poster series covering 19 major

117

figures in the discovery of electricity. Altogether, 22 films listed in the catalogue have a practical application in the laboratory ranging from *Discovering Electricity*, which traces the story of electricity from the earliest time and *What is Electricity?*, through a series on *Basic Electrical Principles* (eight films in all on electrical terms, effects, circuitry and connection and the like) to current research and safety.

The resources on gas consist of 11 films/videocassettes available from the Viscom Film Library. All are in colour and of a duration commensurate with maintaining interest on what are detailed scientific topics where pupils' concentration is apt to wander. Their usefulness and interest is heightened by using presenters such as Paddy Feeney from the television 'Young Scientist of the Year' programme, cartoons, the humour of Kenneth Williams, and the involvement of science teachers in their initial production and the accompanying teachers' notes. It is no surprise, therefore, that some have won international awards. Topics covered include convection, conduction, radiation, refrigeration, the science of flame, and thermostats, as well as natural gas itself in both its extraction and distribution.

Another area of this subject for which there is a useful range of resources is communication, and the prime source here is Telecom. Both its wall posters and booklets are very well produced, especially the former whose colour presentation is second to none. These include a series of four on *Satellite Communication*: (a) *Satellite Launch*; (b) *Goonhilly Earth Station*; (c) *A Telephone Call* and (d) *The World Receives*; *The Post Office Tower*; *A Partial View of a Strowger Automatic Telephone Exchange*, *Post Office Worldwide Telecommunications* and *A History of the Telephone Instrument* with some smaller posters covering the routing of calls, a cross-section of a city street showing the services therein, and the parts of a telephone.

In order to demonstrate the quality of this material it is worth examining one of the posters in question. *Satellite Communication: a satellite launch* depicts four themes in full colour and is clearly annotated in bold print. These comprise a picture of an Atlas Centaur rocket with its various stages, three pictures of the trajectories/orbits, detail of the satellite in synchronous equatorial orbit and an illustration of an Intelsat IV satellite. Thus the poster represents simply and clearly what in fact could be a complicated process explained orally. Another good example is the one entitled *Post Office Worldwide Telecommunications*, which is a large world map with the countries delineated in one of four colours for clarity. The information on cable stations and cable communication links is conveyed by the use of any of 12 permanent symbols. Supplementing this are three smaller maps showing the more intensive communication pattern of North and Southern England and the

Mediterranean area.

Turning from wall posters to the six booklets of Telecom, one finds here a resource of great value for project work. The titles include *Radio and the Post Office—a booklet for students*, which traces the history of the medium with lavish use of colour and black and white illustrations, including facsimile photographs and newspaper headings; *System 'X'—the complete approach to telecommunications*, an account of future systems using micro-electronic technology, with the follow-up benefit of further communication sources such as GEC and Plessey, and *Telecommunication Projects, Names and Dates for Students*, an excellent check-list of the great names in this field, together with important dates and events.

A few films on telecommunications are available from Cable and Wireless Ltd, and Standard Telephones and Cables Ltd. The first company has titles on the laying of submarine telephone/telegraph cables and the building of satellite earth stations around the world. The second company, on the other hand, besides similar titles on cable laying, also has examples covering the intricacies of terminal equipment and post office telephones. Most of these films are in colour and, being fairly technical in nature, are suitable for the more academic.

There is a noticeable lack of films, indeed material of any sort, on ultra-modern communication processes involving the latest technology, whether in fibre optics or the microprocessor field. In view of the rapid changes taking place, this is perhaps not surprising. However, the firms responsible here have a poor record in public relations/educational material, so it cannot be assumed that low-cost material will be made available.

Technical Studies

This subject, essentially practical in nature, does contain an element of theory for which a range of existing low-cost resources can prove useful, if only to reinforce and supplement textbook information, or to provide an interesting change in the teaching programme. It must be borne in mind that there is usually a preponderance of the less academic students involved in this subject and this, combined with the fact that sessions count more than one period, taking up perhaps a whole afternoon, can make the session a testing time for both the teacher's and pupils' concentration. To have some posters or wallcharts to pore over or a film to end the lesson with could make all the difference to the attitude of the class.

For convenience it is worth considering the resources under two headings—woodwork and metalwork, which, to all intents and purposes, embraces workshop technology, concluding with a section on films.

Woodwork resources

The two largest manufacturers of woodworking tools, Record Ridgway and Stanley, have their own education services promoting a range of resources—posters, audiovisual aids, booklets and technical services for teachers. To some extent their services are similar, but as they are both so useful it is of value to consider them each in turn for comparative purposes.

The material available from Record Ridgway is concerned with tools and their uses and this takes the form of annotated wallcharts, posters, including A4 size suitable for photocopying, instruction booklets and five videotapes ranging from 9-25 minutes in length. All in all these resources cover the selection, care, maintenance, safety in use and application of tools. In addition, the firm offers a free lecture and practical demonstration service of all its tools.

While the above firm offers its entire resources free, the same cannot be said for Stanley Tools. However, the charges are small and the material worthy of consideration as it covers different aspects of the subject, or otherwise covers it in greater depth.

First of all are the wallcharts published as two sets, with five in each. The themes are more comprehensive than those of Record Ridgway, including the use of joints and working practices, with such examples as *Frame Construction, How to Cut and Clean a Shoulder* and *Securing Two Pieces of Wood*. Like those of the former company they are also available in A4 size for pupil use and come with full sanction to photocopy. Five background booklets can also be obtained, free of charge, dealing with woodwork principles in an imaginative way rather than simply dwelling on the mechanics of the job; *Man and Measure* and *Man Makes Hole* are two examples.

The three books published by Stanley—*The Stanley Book of Designs for Home Storage, How to Work with Tools and Wood*—a pocket book with dozens of illustrations, and basic illustrations in the use of tools, and the *Stanley Guide to Modern Woodworking Tools* with simple to follow instructions on the basic needs of a good tool kit are all excellent low cost material. All have lively succinct texts accompanying the profuse illustrations, making them easy for pupils to understand.

Of use to the school when setting up a workshop or even as a checklist is the free *Stanley Schedule*, a new and definitive list of necessary tools for the department, all the more invaluable as all the latest equipment is included.

Two free films are also available on planes and Stanley's patented tools. As in the case of Record Ridgway, free technical demonstrations are available, although aimed at teachers rather than pupils.

In conclusion, details of the Stanley *Link* magazine are worth including, despite the fact that its cost puts it beyond the scope of this book. Single copies can, however, be purchased. With contributions from many facets of the education world, full colour presentation with a pull-out wallchart, it has a theme of creativity, innovation and invention, and certainly provides a refreshing look at technical studies in the light of current trends, when the subject has broadened in scope to encompass craft, design and technology.

Information on types of wood, wood products and, to some extent, its applications, is available from three major sources—the Timber Research and Development Association (TRADA); the Fibre Building Board Development Organisation (FIDOR), and the Forestry Commission.

The Timber Research and Development Association is the foremost organization in timber technology and despite its work being essentially for the trade, it can provide some excellent resources in the form of low-cost publications. Information about itself is also of paramount importance, and this, together with details of all its materials, are found in its catalogues.

The Association's wallcharts are worth examining in detail. *How a Tree Grows* depicts the tree with cross sections removed to show the different processes involved in its growth, followed by other diagrams illustrating the process in greater detail. *Seasoning* illustrates, by section drawings, how wood loses moisture and the effects of seasoning upon it—both the techniques of air and kiln seasoning are demonstrated while *Joints in Cabinet Work* shows 16 different joints, including those in solid timber, particle board and plywood. These are just three of 20, all of which are produced for students studying timber from its source to the completed article. Needless to say, the authority behind them is second to none.

Following on from these are free and low-cost booklets on such topics as timber preservation, its source, uses and finishes, and the care, handling and safety of tools as well as a wide-ranging bibliography useful for selecting recommended low-cost items from other sources.

The Association is also the best source for timber specimens, 40 in all, each labelled with its common and botanical name and country of origin.

The Fibre Building Board Development Organisation is the central co-ordinating body for the trade offering advice and information on the use of hardboard and insulating board as well as a range of free teaching aids for schools. These include wallcharts, booklets and samples. The wallcharts are produced in two series, the first dealing with the manufacture, use and application of the material, the second providing more advanced information on the principles of using wood in particular situations and their contribution to thermal insulation and sound control. Though they are only in two-tone colour, they present the information clearly and concisely; this is also true of the booklet dealing with suggested projects for pupils. These include a bedside unit, magazine/record unit, bathroom cabinet and perpetual calendar. The sample boards available are neatly packaged, and ideal for demonstration purposes, each being clearly labelled as to type and thickness.

It is useful to mention the other free publications of this organization which deal with projects that can be undertaken with fibreboard around the home or in a general building context. The whole aspect of insulation is very much in vogue and is well covered, even if only for comparisons. Schools undertaking community project work could find them very useful with the many ideas and practical schemes put forward.

Finally to the Forestry Commission which has amongst its many publications two excellent free booklets—*Notes on Tree Species in Great Britain* and a *Guide to Home Grown Timber*. The first is illustrated, albeit in black-and-white, and deals with where trees (20 in all) are found, the kind of timber each provides, the uses, the age of maturing and height of the species. The second provides the reader with even more detailed information, this time in tabulated form for easy reference and includes details of weight, durability, preservation, treatment and seasoning. The usefulness of this material lies in the fact that it is related to the history of English furniture and especially how styles have developed in particular regions.

Metalwork and workshop technology

These subjects have broadened in scope considerably over the last few years, with greater emphasis being placed on project work involving both theoretical and practical workshop skills. If anything, the subject is more academic and at the higher level becomes a facet of 'A' level Science, especially where combining scientific principles and design criteria in the actual building of a model takes place. In fact, in educational terms, this can be referred to as Project Technology or Control Engineering.

However, regardless of the terminology in use, it is appropriate to include all relevant resources in this section as the Technical Studies Department still has the major say in policy planning. With a short fall in engineering students in higher education and the greater emphasis placed on this subject by the government and the Department of Education and

Science, an examination of the resources available is more than relevant at this time.

Paramount amongst these resources is the journal *School Technology* published by the National Centre for Science and Technology at Trent Polytechnic. This body is also responsible for the *Directory of Resource Material for Teachers of Technology in Schools* as well as its own excellent teaching materials. The journal, published quarterly, is the primary source of current news and comments on the subject covering such aspects as curriculum innovation, examples of work undertaken in various schools, and resources. It has a policy of including articles from only practising educationalists. Each issue contains tried and tested details of its own resources ranging from equipment construction guides through technology models to project technology handbooks, on such topics as *Engine Test Beds* and *Muzzle Furnaces.* All publications are low-cost or reasonably priced and are such that they can be used as a basis for individual lessons or a complete course if need be involving a whole new curriculum. And with the *Directory of Resource Material for Teachers of Technology in Schols* it is possible to supplement the Centre's material with a wide range from other sources, at low-cost. It is not surprising to find that the directory is published in the form of a computer print-out with the 80 major reference headings for sources, listed in alphabetical order. It is disappointing, however, that the last major up-date was in 1976, though it must be said that most references do hold good especially those listing free items. All kinds of material is listed, films, pamphlets and charts with the major topics, for which low-cost items are available, being metals, aspects of engineering and mechanics (tools, gears, motors, vehicles of all types), ships, bridges and railways. It will be as well to comment on those resources which have a general application in most schools and these will invariably involve engines, mechanical components and principles.

British Petroleum publishes 20 low-cost colour wallcharts available at a discount to schools, covering all aspects of engine components and mechanics. Text is kept to a minimum relying on a series of pictures to convey the often complicated processes involved. With such titles as *The Principles of the Four Star Diesel, The Flywheel Magneto* and *A Typical Lubrication System*, the world of engines is brought to life in such a way that pupils of all abilities should be able to understand it. The series, until recently, also incorporated titles dealing with nuts, washers and locking methods, drills and other metalworking tools as well as threads, but these appear to be permanently out of print.

Perkins Engines of Peterborough have a wide selection of free colour posters available on different types of engines and their application.

For more detailed information on the mechanics of engines those firms who specialize in components can be contacted: Lucas Electrical for electronics, Girling for brake systems and Champion for spark plugs. Handbooks, workshop manuals and charts can all be obtained, gratis, as the majority of firms in this field have material which, if not originally designed for schools, is for the trade on an instructional theme.

As a good example, Champion makes five free publications available. *Automotive Technical Service Manual* is a 40-page book full of highly technical information presented in an interesting and simple way by the lavish use of colour diagrams and a well-spaced planned text. Besides the basic role of the spark plug, topics such as engine efficiency, the ignition and fuel system, and fuel economy are also included. It is interesting to note that the publication lists in its acknowledgements the assistance of a major automobile magazine and a renowned car manual publisher.

Facts About Spark Plugs and Engines: (a) *Automobiles* and (b) *Motor Cycles*, are two booklets covering in some depth, yet in a readable way, supplemented liberally with diagrams, the role of this vital component and the problems that can be encountered. Indirectly they convey useful information on fault finding and the efficient running of engines as well as hints on safety.

Finally to the two colour charts, one useful for purposes of definition, the other for class use, each showing spark plug conditions with explanations alongside. There is also a fault finder diagram on the rear of the smaller chart which includes all possible problems that can be encountered with an engine—not just electrical faults. Ten symptoms the engine may show can be simply checked off in the diagram with any of 14 possible causes on the chart.

Films

There are two excellent free films recently produced on the subject of design technology available from the Central Film Library. The first is *Let's Make a Model*, designed to make 15-18 year-old students think about some of the modelling techniques available to the engineer and technologist today; the other, *Engineering in Schools*, shows the development of a variety of projects undertaken by three schools, showing designing, research, production and the problems encountered.

The Central Film Library is, in fact, the largest source of material on the use and techniques of metalworking tools, having only recently published a separate catalogue listing those films of importance. Most, however, cost in excess of five pounds each to hire, so it is necessary to go elsewhere for free titles. Guild Sound and Vision, in its classified catalogue on Engineering, Industry and Mining, has a small number of appropriate free films such as *Choosing the Right Tool, Know the Drill* and *Eclipse Means Quality*. It has, on the other hand, a wide range of films on different aspects depicting the engineer and processes involved in the factory, placing the skills obtained in the workshop in the context of the outside world.

Autolock and Deadlock Milling Systems shows two famous milling systems alongside competing processes and by the use of slow-motion sequences of the milling cutter on different materials and animation for demonstrating the basic principles involved, the film is ideal for illustrating to pupils the principles of various milling systems. *Power From Precision*, produced by Association Engineers Ltd, one of the world's largest manufacturers of precision components for the aerospace, automotive, engineering and marine industries, demonstrates how precision products are manufactured through advanced techniques. *Profile for Productivity* illustrates how tools are made and used by leading engineering companies and *A Tool of Quality* centres on producing the right kind of steel for a particular job.

Next are those films on particular aspects of mechanical work and here we have an excellent source in the major oil companies such as Shell. This company has 11 titles of possible use, dealing with such topics as gears, hydraulics, lubrication, forging and the principles of how engines work. All are in colour and while some were produced over 15 years ago, their content is still relevant. Burmah, Castrol and Esso also produce useful films to supplement the above, especially on the functions of lubricating oil.

Other relevant films are three from David Brown Tractors with such self-explanatory titles as *Selectamatic Hydraulics Troubleshooting, Tractor Hydraulics Explained* and *Keep Your Tractor Fit*. The content of these could be applied to any make of diesel engine.

The number and variety of films is such that it is possible to arrange a programme for the whole of the school year for a particular class. Most topics within Technical Studies can be included and, for example, in the case of a fifth form group, could provide excellent revision material. Also, they could, as mentioned at the start of this section, be an excellent way to round off a long practical session in the workshop.

5

Conclusion

Incorporating low-cost and free material in the school library calls for some kind of acquisitions and organizations policy. Despite the name tag of these resources, costs inevitably are incurred whether in terms of postage or time spent in writing letters as well as in scanning relevant literature for sources of new material.

Acquisition policy

Each school will therefore have to decide for itself what is the best course to follow, bearing in mind the various subjects taught, existing library provision, annual budget and staffing quota. While it is the author's experience that some schools have sent off for as much of this material as they could, because their library was in such a parlous state, such action contradicts one of the fundamental qualities of low-cost material—that of currency. It should in general only be obtained as and when required, where one knows it will prove of greatest benefit. The very nature of the material dictates in many instances that it is only available at the good will of the organization and it would be an abuse to use it merely to build up the stock of the library, though where multiple copies of material are available it is worth acquiring the maximum stated.

Co-operation with subject departments is essential if duplication is to be avoided, especially when dealing with material applicable in more than one area. A knowledge and understanding of the curriculum as it affects each department's information requirements is desirable, while it would be ideal for the librarian to be involved in the planning of new courses from the start—to offer advice on potential material.

A careful check should be made of sources contacted whether by oneself or by a pupil or member of staff. A card index kept for the purpose could contain the name of the organization, its address, where it was first mentioned as a source, the date a letter was sent and when a reply was received, the type of material received, whether a catalogue was available, the relevance of the material and so on. Any lists or catalogues of resources should be filed for reference in the library, and only photocopies of them handed to staff. It is wise to treat the resources themselves in the same way. Close monitoring of all material is essential, as it may stimulate a greater response than was expected.

Organization

Considering the context in which low-cost material is useful—that of projects—then perhaps its physical organization is best done through the use of box files, arranged in classified order under subject headings relevant to the topic where it proves of most worth. Posters and wallsheets are best filed separately, however, under broad subject areas. The content of the resources area will be changing in line with the curriculum and to a large extent renewed annually. Within this period some of the material could be on extended loan to a class or set, only presenting itself with the problem of storage on its return, when in fact it could be out of date, which leads to the other major problem—when to discard. The rule here must be only to discard when the material's updated counterpart has been obtained.

Details of the resources should appear in the library catalogue under the appropriate Dewey number, users being guided by subject headings, the author finding those produced by his County Library (Schools section) quite satisfactory for the purpose. An indication of where the material is actually located is essential, especially if it is not to be found in the main body of the library. The amount of cross-references in the catalogue will depend on the time and staff available and the efficacy of embarking on any such detailed programme. Time might be better spent compiling lists of relevant sources on particular topics where individuals could themselves obtain material, noting new releases of films and videocassettes on free loan, or providing news-sheets about new material added to the library.

The whole aspect of low-cost and free material lends itself to instilling in pupils the skills required in obtaining information, as many of their general interests are served by the sources available. Topics of interest to boys for which there is copious material include agriculture (tractors and machinery), aircraft, the armed services, camping, cars, fishing, football, guns, lorries and motorcycles. For the girls there is childcare and nursing, cooking, fashion, horses, pets and pop music.

The library may 'give' pupils spare copies of resources in return for the cost of postage; pupils may then swap items with one another. All this helps to improve the library's image amongst pupils and may well encourage pupils to offer resources to the library when interest has waned. Pupils gain confidence in contacting external sources for information and, of course, are made aware of their existence. Pupils who obtain the information for themselves are far more likely to treat the collections of others with greater consideration, also considerable pressure can be taken off the library when pupils can use their own material for class projects.

Promotion of the library

Film shows

Film shows can be arranged by the library showing those titles of a more entertaining nature. Topics here could include motor and motorcycle racing, aircraft, fishing, horse riding, travel, wildlife and pets. If not forming the basis of a weekly programme through the winter months then selected titles could be booked for end of term 'treats'. The fact that many films are booked for months if not a year ahead only goes to show how popular they are and makes them all the more worthy of consideration.

School bookshops

Instilling in pupils the pleasure of book ownership can be done through a school bookshop—the organization of which can be aided through the excellent services of the School Bookshop Association. If the library takes on the responsibility of this and runs one alongside its other facilities the extra stock can add a whole new dimension for its clients and, at least as far as browsing is concerned, can be seen to be supplementing existing provision. This could prove a boon for the time-tabled library lesson when an ever-changing assortment of titles in a library which has few new additions to stock can offer fresh scope especially to those pupils whose reading interests need to be stimulated. The scheme operated by W H Smith where books are changed regularly is an excellent example of schemes which booksellers have developed in recent years.

Book fairs

From the bookshop one can graduate to the book fair which is increasingly being used as a means of giving pupils the chance to become acquainted with the world of books as well as being a money-raising effort usually organized by schools' parent teacher associations. The local supplier, in this case, will provide as much stock as he has available for a short period, probably no more than a week, with a discount of perhaps 10% on those books sold. The stock can be supplemented with books sent by publishers, arranged through their area representatives or through the Educational Publishers Council who will contact publishers on the school's behalf. If the book fair is seen to be a good publicity venture then it is possible that the publishers will in fact donate a number of books for the library.

Literature and the promotion of fiction

There is much free material available from publishers (and their representatives) and booksellers—posters, spare copies of book jackets, and promotion leaflets which can be used to publicize authors and support displays in the school library. Articles from the colour supplements, the Radio Times and TV Times can also provide useful display and resource material. Examples include those relating to K M Peyton's *Flambards*, the *Worzel Gummidge* books and Waugh's *Brideshead Revisited.*

Microcomputers

Despite the current economic situation, there is one expanding area in education at the present time. In 1981 the government announced that every secondary school would have a microcomputer—and these have enormous potential in terms of dealing with the physical processes involved in locating, identifying and assessing low-cost and free material.

Already research is underway in this field with the system known as SIR (School Information Retrieval), the project being carried out by the Research Department of Aslib in collaboration with Kent-Barlow Information Associates. The machine found most popular with schools is the Research Machine RML 380Z microcomputer, and this is the one chosen for the experiment. The first demonstration database includes about 500 items on current world problems, mainly of an environmental nature, an area where low-cost and free material proliferates.

The card index discussed at the beginning of this chapter could be replaced by a computerized system. Pupils and staff would then be able to find out quickly what was available and most suitable for their own individual requirements. The use a particular school made of this information could be the basis of its own data bank and information system.

On a more general level, information on the free and low-cost material is already appearing on Prestel—the Health Education Council being a good example. The scope for expanding this provision is enormous if the information providers, as identified in this book, are prepared to put up the data.

Conclusion

Recommendations

The main purpose of this book has been to show how schools can make the best possible use of limited funds at a time of great financial stringency. When work on it began, funds were far from plentiful. Now, six years later, the situation is worse and seems unlikely to improve in the foreseeable future. By attempting to demonstrate that high quality resource material can be acquired economically from a wide variety of reliable sources, it is hoped that other school librarians will be encouraged to devise a strategy for themselves, in order to supplement more conventional material. With possible forthcoming changes in the 16+ examination, there are likely to be continuing demands on the resource organization in schools. Each school must develop its own policy in resource provision. The library must continue to make the best use of the money available by utilizing professional skills to the utmost. The fact that Western democratic society depends on a free flow of information for its survival should ensure a ready supply of low-cost and free material that can be acquired from near and far. With imagination, initiative and enterprise, and perhaps with the help of the new information technology, the librarian must continue to provide the best possible service—low-cost and free material of the kind discussed in this book could make all the difference to the quality of the service.

Bibliography

ALLAN, Margaret. *The School Library Resource Centre.* Crosby Lockwood Staples, 1976. p165.

Association of Agriculture. *A Bibliography of Sources for the Use of Teachers and Teachers in Training.* 1979. p132.

BESWICK, Barbara. 'Library provision for sixth and seventh year students in a rural comprehensive school'. *Education Libraries Bulletin,* 23(1), Spring, 1980. pp15-22.

BESWICK, Norman W. *Organising Resources—six case studies.* Heinemann Educational Books, 1975. p369.

BESWICK, Norman W. *School Resource Centres.* Evans/Methuen Educational, 1972. pp103.

BOLWELL, L and LINES, C. 'Teaching history and resources for local studies in primary and middle schools: an inservice experiment'. *Teaching History,* 2(8), November, 1972. pp320-6.

BRADMAN, Tony. 'When you can no longer beg or borrow...buy'. *Guardian,* 19th May, 1981. p11.

BRAKE, Terence. 'Educating for access into the information culture'. *Education Libraries Bulletin,* 23(2), Summer, 1980. pp1-14.

BRAKE, Terence. *The Need to Know: teaching the importance of information.* (Report No.5511). British Library Research and Development Department, 1980. p81.

BRAKE, Terence. 'The need to know—teaching the importance and use of information at school'. *Education Libraries Bulletin,* 22(2), Summer, 1979. pp38-51.

BRIAULT, Dr E. *Allocation and Management of Resources in Schools.* Council for Educational Technology for the United Kingdom, 1974. p49.

BRICE, Jennifer. 'School librarianship'. *New Library World,* 80(946), April, 1979. pp68-71.

BRYANT, Margaret. 'Documentary and study materials for teachers and pupils'. *Teaching History,* 1(3), May, 1970. pp194-202.

Bibliography

COLTHURST, C.J.S. *Towards a Resource Centre: parts I and II.* Lancing College, 1972. p45.

COOPER, Helen. *Wallsheets—choosing and making.* National Committee for Audio-visual Aids in Education, 1971. p36.

DAVIES, W.J.K. *Learning Resources? An Argument for Schools.* Council for Educational Technology for the United Kingdom, 1975. p108.

Department of Education and Science. *Aspects of Secondary Education in England: a survey by HM Inspector of Schools.* HMSO, 1980. p312.

Department of Education and Science. *Bulletin,* May, 1981. (Ref 7/81) p10.

Department of Education and Science. *The School Curriculum.* HMSO, 1981. p20.

Design Council. *Design Resources for Teachers.* 1976. p32.

DYER, C, BROWN, R and GOLDSTEIN, E.D. *School Libraries: theory and practice.* Clive Bingley, 1970. p181.

Educational Publishers Council. *Lucky Child?* EPC, 1978. (Leaflet)

Educational Publishers Council. *Publishing for Schools.* EPC, 1977. p56.

Exley Publications Ltd. Free stuff for kids. 1982.

GUNDREY, Elizabeth. *250 more things to send off for.* Beaver Books, 1981. p110.

HANSON, J. *The Use of Resources.* George Allen and Unwin Ltd, 1975. p108.

HERRING, James E. *Teaching Library Skills in Schools.* NFER, 1978. p96.

HOLDER, M L and MITSON, R. *Resource Centres.* Methuen Educational, 1974. p66.

HOLLAND, P. *Quangos: a definitive survey.* P Holland at the House of Commons. 1979.

Institute of Public Relations. *Register of Members—1978.* 1978. p104.

LAST, Derick. 'Fairer distribution'. (Regional co-ordination of the production of resources). *The Times Educational Supplement,* 29th May, 1981. p35.

LINDSAY, John. 'Information training in secondary schools'. *Education Libraries Bulletin,* 19(3), Autumn, 1976. pp16-21.

LONGWORTH, N. *Information in the Secondary School Curricula.* M.Phil. thesis. Southampton University, 1976. (Unpublished).

MITSON, R. *The Resources Centre, Codsall.* Codsall Comprehensive School, 1972. p15.

MORBY, G. *Knowhow: a guide to information, training and campaigning materials for information and advice workers.* Community Information Project. British Library Research and Development Publications, 1979. p182.

National Book League. *Books for Schools.* 1978. p70.

National Committee for Audio-visual Aids in Education. *The Organisation of*

Bibliography

Audio-visual Resources for Learning in a Local Educational Authority. 1970. p27.

NETTLE, S. 'The libraries that lend on borrowed time'. *Guardian,* 6th March, 1981. p11.

PARTINGTON, Lena. *The European Communities: a guide to the literature, and an indication of sources of information.* Department of the Environment, 1974. p101.

PASSMORE, Biddy. 'Surveys of libraries to be published'. *The Times Educational Supplement,* 9th May, 1980. p3.

PAYNE, P and WILLETT, I. *Information Services in Education: an inventory of organisations and associations in the UK providing information services relevant to education.* Lancaster University Centre for Educational Research and Development, 1978. p81.

PEEL, Harold. 'A survival kit for teaching geography in a resources desert'. *Teaching Geography,* 3(3), January, 1978. pp132-3.

RADDON, Rosemary. 'Stocking a school library'. *School Librarian,* 26(4), December 1978. pp315-8.

RICHARDSON, Nigel. 'Feature probe is a classroom winner'. *The Times Educational Supplement,* 13th October, 1978. p28.

ROGERS, Rick. 'Asking nicely. Facts and how to find them'. *Guardian,* 12th June, 1981. p11.

School Bookshop Association. *How to Set up and Run a School Bookshop.* 1981, p42.

Schoolmaster Publishing Company Ltd. *Treasure Chest for Teachers: services available to teachers and schools.* 1977. p203.

Southern Regional Council for Further Education. *A Source Book of Visual Aids Material for the Teaching of Commerce.* 1967. p23.

STOLL, Martin. *Fun for Free.* Armada, 1981. p128.

SURRIDGE, Owen. 'Books with a limited shelf life'. *Guardian,* 2nd June, 1981. p11.

THORPE, Stephen. 'Leaflets and libraries'. *New Library World,* 80(947), May 1979. pp86-7.

Understanding British Industry Resource Centre. *Teaching Materials.* 1977. p11.

WAITE, Clifford and COLEBOURNE, Ronald. *Not By Books Alone: a symposium on library resources in schools.* School Library Association, 1975. p124.

WILSON, R.W. *Useful Addresses for Science Teachers.* Edward Arnold (Publishers) Ltd, 1974. p554.

WINSLADE, B A J and BESWICK, N W. *Resource Centres: an annotated bibliography.* College of Librarianship Wales, 1972. p44.

WRAGG, Prof E C. 'Superteach and the Dinosaurs'. (The radical development of teaching tactics from 1960 onwards). *Guardian,* 9th January, 1979. p9.

Bibliography

YOUNG, M. *Innovation and Research in Education*. Routledge & Kegan Paul, 1965. p184.

Youth in Society. 'Development Education Resources, a selective listing of relevant agencies publications, visual material, games and simulations'. 82. September, 1983. pp22-3.

Appendix 1

The following books provide addresses of the major firms, organizations, and institutions.

Agricultural Press *Farm and Garden Equipment Guide* 1980
Alan Armstrong and Associates Ltd *5001 Hard to Find Publishers and their Addresses* 1982

Boag, J (editor) *Willings Press Guide* T Skinner 1983

Contact *The UK News Contact Directory* 1983

Dunning, R *Local Sources for the Young Historian.* Muller 1973

Fairbairn, R (editor) *Motor Cycle and Cycle Trader Year Book* Wheatlands Journals Ltd 1982
Family Welfare Association *Charities Digest* 1983
Floyd, R C (editor) *Motor Specifications and Prices* Stone & Cox 1978

Henderson, G P & Henderson, S P A *Directory of British Associations and Associations in Ireland.* CBD Research 1980

IPC Transport Press Ltd *Motor Trader Directory* 1979

James, T M *Sources of Teaching Aids and Facilities for Teachers of Catering, Home Economics and Related Subjects* Edward Arnold 1976

Kelly's Directories *Kelly's Post Office London Directory* 1983
Kelly's Directories *Kelly's Manufacturers and Merchants Directory* 1984
Kemps Group *The British Clothing Industry Year Book 1983* 1983

Appendix 1

Lonsbury, A   *See Britain at Work: A whole world of fascinating visits to craft workshops and factories*   Exley Publications   1981

Macdonald & Janes Publishers Ltd   *Angling Times Yearbook*   1982
Millard, P (editor)   *Trade Associations and Professional Bodies of the UK*   Pergamon   1979
Morgan-Grampian Book Publishing Co Ltd   *Travel Trade Directory*   1983

National Food and Drink Federation   *Food and Drink Handbook*   1980
Newham Books Ltd   *Food Trades Directory and Food Buyers Yearbook 1983–84*   1983

Pettit, R   *The Craft Business*   Pitman Publishing   1975

Roope, W A C (editor)   *Municipal Yearbook 1983*   Municipal Publications Ltd   1983

Segal, A (editor)   *Careers Encyclopedia*   Cassell   1980
Shipley, P (editor)   *Directory of Pressure Groups and Representative Associations*   Bowker Publicity Co Ltd, London   1979
Summerson, E J   *Careers Information and Careers Libraries*   Careers Consultants Ltd   1979

Whitaker   *Whitaker's Almanac*   1984
Wilson, R W   *Useful Addresses for Science Teachers*   Edward Arnold   1974
Wright, R T   *Source Book for Agricultural Education*   Moray House College of Education   1966

Appendix 2

Sources of information about low-cost and free material

The following sources have proved useful in the preparation of this book. The majority issue annual lists of resources. Periodicals are noted by an asterisk (*) and frequency of publication is given.

Agriculture and Fisheries (Ministry of)   *Sectional List*   HMSO
Arts Council Information Bulletin   Arts Council of GB   Bi-monthly
Arts Council of Great Britain   *Publications List, 1978–9*   Annual
Arts Documentation Monthly   Arts Council of GB   Monthly
Arts Review   Richard Gainsborough Periodicals Ltd   Fortnightly
Association for Science Education   *ASE and SNS Publications*

Bank Education   *BES Teachers Resources*
Berry, Peter S (compiler)   *Guide to Resources in Environmental Education*
    Conservation Trust
Birmingham City Museum and Art Gallery   *Guides and Catalogues*
Botanical Society of the British Isles   *Stock List*
British Council of Churches   *Guide to Project Work in Religious Studies;*
    Publications List
British Farm Produce Council   *Leaflets and Books: available free*
British Goat Society   *List of Publications*
British Industrial and Scientific Film Association   *BISFA Presenting the British*
    Industrial and Sponsored Film Awards Annual (Describes new films entered
    for awards and thus gives indication of recently released titles)
British Museum Publications   *Books in Print; Natural History Publications;*
    Postcards
British Nutrition Foundation   *Publications; Visual Aids: food and nutrition*
British Petroleum Educational Service   *Resources Catalogue for Teachers*
British Trades Alphabet Ltd   *BTA Study Cards*
Building Societies Association   *Teaching Aids*

Careers Research and Advisory Centre   *CRAC Publications Catalogue and Price List*

Central Office of Information   *Sectional List*   HMSO

Central Office of Information (Reference Division)   *The Commonwealth: a guide to material and information available to schools and to the public*

Central Office of Information   *Sales List of Reference Documents; Services Available to the UK Public*

Centre for Alternative Technology   *Publications*

Centre for World Development Education   *Catalogue; Development Education: a guide to agency sources and sources in UK*

Christian Aid   *General Publications and Visual Aids*

Christian Education Movement   *CEM Publications Catalogue*

City Communications Centre   *City Brief: educational information*

Commission for Racial Equality   *Education for Multi-cultural Society: audio-visual aids for teachers; Education for a Multi-cultural Society: a bibliography for teachers; Film Catalogue: community and race relations*

Commission of the European Communities   *European Commission: publications available free; The European Community: a brief reading list*

Community Service Volunteers Advisory Service   *Learn Through Caring Publications*

Conservation Trust   *Information Sheet*

Council for Education in World Citizenship   *United Nations and World Studies Materials; World Studies Resource Guide*

Council for Environmental Education   *Bibliographies; Conservation: some sources of information; Directory of Environmental Literature and Teaching Aids; Environmental Education Enquiries* (2nd edition); *Publications List*

Council for Nature   *Publications*

Council of Subject Teaching Associations   *Brochures*

Department of Education and Science   *Environmental Education: sources of information for teachers; Free Publications: order form and publications list; International Understanding: sources of information on international organisations 1979. A handbook for schools and colleges*

Department of Industry Education Publicity Office   *Films on Engineering for Schools*

Design Council   *Design Centre Shop Mail Order Book List*

Earth Resources Research Ltd   *ERR Publications List*

Electricity Council   *Understanding Electricity: a catalogue of educational material and facilities for schools and colleges made available by the electricity supply industry in the UK, the Republic of Ireland and by the UK Atomic Energy Authority*

Environmental Group Information Service   *EGIS Education Teaching Aids for Environmental Studies*

Forbes Publishing Ltd   *Teaching Aids* (Annual supplement to the Home Economics magazine)

Forestry Commission   *Books and Periodicals on Forestry and Allied Subjects;*
Catalogue of Publications; Sectional List   HMSO
Friends of the Earth Ltd   *Books from Friends of the Earth; Campaign Material*

General Dental Council   *Catalogue of Dental Health*
Goethe Institute (Manchester-German Cultural Institute for Northern England)
Audio-visual Library Catalogue
Greater London Council   *Directory of Information Sources in the GLC*
Greater London Council Bookshop   *GLC Publications List*
Guardian: Education Guardian   Guardian Newspapers Ltd   Tuesdays
Guonghwa Company   *General Catalogue No 5* (The leading importer of pub-
lications from China, many in English)

Health Education Council   *Nutrition Education Publications and Teaching Aids*
Source List; Resources Folder; Smoking and Health Publications and Teaching
Aids: source list
Help the Aged Education Department   *Education Materials*
Her Majesty's Stationery Office   *Books for Schools; Find Out About the Coun-
try with HMSO Books; A List of Publications on the Home and Family*
Historical Association   *Publications*

Institute of Geological Sciences   *Publications of the Institute of Geological*
Sciences: a brief guide to the publications of the Institute
International Wool Secretariat   *List of Educational Material*

Lake District National Park Centre   *Youth and Schools Service Publications*
List
Landmans Bookshop Ltd   *Catalogue of Books and Pamphlets on Farming, Gar-
dening and Forestry*
Lawn Tennis Association   *Books, Booklets, Journals, Charts and Films Recom-
mended by the Lawn Tennis Association*
London Tourist Board   *Information*
Lonsdale, M K (editor)   *Charities Digest*

Manpower Services Commission   *COIC Catalogue of Careers Films and Other*
Audio-visual Aids
Manpower Services Commission Careers and Occupational Information Centre
COIC Literature
Ministry of Overseas Development   *Overseas Development and Aid: a guide*
to sources of material

National Association for Environmental Education   *Publications*
National Association for Maternal and Child Welfare   *Child Health and*
Development Books for Parents, Teachers, Students; Publications
National Children's Bureau   *Spotlight on Sources of Information About Chil-
dren*
National Christian Education Movement   *NCEC Catalogue*

National Committee for Audio-visual Aids in Education *Visual Education Year Book*

National Dairy Council *Catalogue of Educational Material*

National Documentation Centre for sport, physical education and recreation *Some Bibliographies etc on Sport and the Handicapped*

National Farmers Union *National Farmers Union Publications for Sale*

National Gallery *National Gallery Books and Catalogues; National Gallery Colour Postcards*

Nature Conservancy Council Library *Information Sheet No 1: maps, posters and wallcharts on British natural history and ecology*

Nature Conservancy Council *Postal Sales Price List and Order Form*

Occidental Group Education Service *Publications on the North Sea Oil Industry*

Overseas Development Institute *Development Guide: a directory of non-commercial organisations in Britain actively concerned in overseas development and training* 3rd edition

Oxfam Education and Youth Department *Oxfam Education and Youth Material*

Pratt, Dr C J *Directory of Resource Material for Teachers of Technology in Schools* National Centre for School Technology

Record Ridgway Education Service *Record Ridgway Education Service for Teachers in Schools and Colleges*

Royal Society for the Prevention of Cruelty to Animals *Slides and Other Educational Materials*

Schools Council with the Health Education Council *Relationship and Sexuality: an annotated selection of publications and teaching aids*

Schools Information Centre on the Chemical Industry *Films: an information booklet* (2nd revised edition); *Some Sources of Information.* Individual sheets on the following: a) Beer and wine making; b) Building materials; c) Colour; d) Cosmetics; e) Detergents; f) Paints; g) Petroleum and North Sea oil; h) Pollution; i) Synthetic fibres; j) Water

Scottish Tourist Board *Books to Help You*

Soil Association *Soil Association Booklist*

Sports Council *Publications Available From the Sports Council and Regional Sports Council*

Stanley Tools Ltd Education Department *Stanley in Education*

Tate Gallery *Tate Gallery Catalogue of Publications, Books, Posters, Colour Prints and Cards*

Timber Research and Development Association *TRADA Publications*

Tourist Board Bookshop *London: useful publications*

Understanding British Industry Resource Centre   *Careers Information: a guide to sources; Schools and Industry: developing the links; Teaching Materials*
United Nations Children's Fund   *UNICEF Education Catalogue*
United Nations Information Centre   *The United Nations on Films: a catalogue of 16mm sound films on the United Nations and the specialized agencies*
United Society for the Propagation of the Gospel   *Resources Folder*
University of Birmingham Sports Documentation Centre   *A List of Some Organisations in Britain Concerned with Sport and the Disabled*

Victoria and Albert Museum   *Sectional List*   HMSO

Williams, G   *Urban and Environmental Studies: a film guide* (Occasional paper No 6)   University of Manchester. Department of Town and Country Planning
World Council of Churches   *Publications*

Youth Bureau   *Sources of Resource Materials*

Appendix 3

Free and low-cost periodicals

Those that bear a small charge are marked with an asterisk (*).

Arts Council Bulletin Information Office, Arts Council of Great Britain, 105 Piccadilly, London W1V 0AM *Bi-monthly*

Atom United Kingdom Atomic Energy Authority, Information Services Branch UKAE, 11 Charles II Street, London SW1Y 4QP *Monthly*

Barclay Trust Money Matters Barclays Bank Ltd, Group Economics Dept, 54 Lombard Street, London EC3 3AH *Quarterly*

Better Times (The Shell Better Britain Company Newsletter) Nature Conservancy Council, PO Box No 6, Huntingdon, Cambs PE18 6BU *Quarterly*

*Bother** Oxfam, 274 Banbury Road, Oxford OX2 7DZ (A monthly comment on poverty and the struggle for development) *Monthly*

BP Shield International The British Petroleum Company PLC, Britannia House, Moor Lane, London EC2Y 9BU *Bi-monthly*

*British Amnesty** Amnesty International, British Section, Tower House, 8-14 Southampton Street, London WC2E 7MF *Bi-monthly*

British Shipping News General Council of British Shipping, 30-32 St Mary Axe, London EC3A 8ET *Bi-monthly*

British Telecom Journal Public Relations Dept, 23 Howland Street, London W1P 6HQ *Quarterly*

*Broadsheet** (Senior and Junior editions) Council for Education in World Citizenship, 43 Russell Square, London WC1B 5DA *Bi-monthly*

BSA Bulletin The Building Societies Association, 34 Park Street, London W1Y 3PF *Quarterly*

Building Society News The Building Societies Association, 34 Park Street, London W1Y 3PF *Monthly*

Bulletin The Polytechnic of North London, Holloway Road, London N7 8OB (Schools Information Centre on the Chemical Industry) *Quarterly*

Appendix 3

Bulletin of Environmental Education * *BEE* Town and Country Planning Association, 17 Carlton House Terrace, London SW1Y 5AS *Monthly*

Castrol News Castrol Educational Division, Dept CB, Blackjack Street, Cirencester *Quarterly*

Cheque In Midland Bank Ltd, 39 Long Acre, London WC2E 9JT *Quarterly*

Consumer News Department of Trade, Information Division, 1 Victoria Street, London SW1H 0ET *Bi-monthly*

Countryside The Countryside Commission, John Dower House, Crescent Place, Cheltenham, Glos *Bi-monthly*

Dairy Education National Dairy Centre, John Princes Street, London W1M 0AP *Quarterly*

Development News Overseas Development Administration, Eland House, Stag Place, London SW1E 5DE *Monthly*

Earth Science Conservation (Nature Conservancy Council) The Geology and Physiography Section, Pearl House, Bartholomew Street, Newbury, Berks *Bi-monthly*

Employment News Department of Employment, 8 St James's Square, London SW1Y 4JB *Bi-monthly*

EP News (European Parliament) 2 Queen Anne's Gate, London SW1H 9AA *Monthly*

Equality Now Overseas House, Quay Street, Manchester M3 3HN *Quarterly*

Esso Magazine Esso Petroleum Co Ltd, Victoria Street, London SW1E 5JW *Quarterly*

Europe 82 (Incorporating Euroforum) Press and Information Office of the European Community, 20 Kensington Palace Gardens, London W8 4QQ *Monthly*

Europe Information External Relations Spokeman's Group and Directorate-General for Information Documentation Service; Bur Berl. 2/84 Commission of the European Communities, Rue de la Loi 200, B-1049 Brussels, Belgium *Monthly*

European File Commission of the European Committee, Director-General for Information, Rue de la Loi 200, B-1049, Brussels *Bi-monthly*

Eurostat News Statistical Office of the European Communities, B-1049 Bruxelles, Bâtiment Berlaymont, Rue de la Loie 200 (Bureau de Liaison) *Quarterly*

Flight Deck * Directoriate of Naval Air Warfare, Ministry of Defence, Whitehall, London SW1 *Quarterly*

Focus Director of Polytechnics, 309 Regent Street, London W1R 7PE *Every four months*

Focus on Thailand Royal Thai Embassy, 30 Queens Gate, London SW7 *Monthly*

Ford News Ford Motor Co Ltd, Eagle Way, Brentwood, Essex *Weekly*

Forum   Directorate of Press and Information, Council of Europe, 67006 Stras-
bourg, Cedex, France   *Monthly*

*Gateway**   Church of England Children's Society, Old Town Hall, Kennington
Road, London SE11 4QD   *Quarterly*
*Globe and Laurel**   Royal Marines, Eastney, Southsea, Hants   *Bi-monthly*

Health Education News   The Health Education Council, 78 New Oxford Street,
London WC1A 1AM   *Bi-monthly*
Heart Bulletin   British Heart Foundation, 57 Gloucester Place, London W1M
4DM   *Quarterly*
Heritage Outlook   Heritage Education Group, 17 Carlton House Terrace,
London SW1Y 5AW   *Quarterly*

Industry/Education View   Department of Industry, Gaywood House, 29 Great
Peter Street, London SW1P 3LW   *Quarterly*

League of Pity News   National Society for the Prevention of Cruelty to Children,
1 Riding House Street, London W1P 8AA   *Quarterly*
*The Lifeboat**   Royal National Lifeboat Institution, West Quay Road, Poole,
Dorset BH15 1HZ   *Quarterly*
The Lion and the Dragon   Regimental Headquarters, The King's Own Royal
Border Regiment, The Castle, Carlisle CA3 8UR   *Half-yearly*
Lloyds Bank Review   Schools Liaison Officer, Lloyds Bank Ltd, PO Box 215,
71 Lombard Street, London EC3P 3BS   *Quarterly*

Midland Bank Review   Public Relations and Advertising Dept, Midland Bank
Ltd, PO Box 2, Griffin House, Silver Street Head, Sheffield S1 3GG   *Quar-
terly*
Money Management Review   Schools Liaison Officer, LOA/ASLO Information
Centre, Buckingham House, 62/63 Queen Street, London EC4R 1AD   *Quar-
terly*
Multiple Sclerosis News   The Multiple Sclerosis Society of Great Britain and
Northern Ireland, 4 Tachbrook Street, London SW1V 1SJ   *Quarterly*

National Westerminster Bank Quarterly Review   National Westminster Bank
Ltd, 41 Lothbury, London EC2P 2BP   *Quarterly*
NATO Review   Central Office of Information, Publications Division (LH511),
Hercules Road, London SE1 7DU   *Bi-monthly*
*Navy News**   HMS Nelson, Portsmouth   *Monthly*
New Equals   Commission for Racial Equality, Elliot House, 10/12 Allington
Street, London SW1E 5EM   *Monthly*
Newscheck   Manpower Services Commission, Careers and Occupation Infor-
mation Centre, 3 St Andrew's Place, London NW1 4LB   *Monthly*
*Newsheet**   Council for Environmental Education, Reading University School
of Education, London Road, Reading RG1 5AQ   *Monthly*

Appendix 3

Newsletter* Council for Environmental Education, Reading University School of Education, London Road, Reading RG1 5AQ *Monthly*

Scala Frankfurter Societates—Druckerei GmbH, Postfach 2929, D-6, Frankfurt/Main 1, Frankerallee 71-81, West Germany *Monthly*

Schools Council News Schools Council, 160 Great Portland Street, London W1N 6LL *Quarterly*

School Technology* NCST, Trent Polytechnic, Burton Street, Nottingham NG1 4BU *Quarterly*

Shell Education News Shell Education Service, Shell-Mex House, Strand, London WC2R 0DX *Every four months*

Soldier Magazine* Clayton Barracks, Aldershot, Hants GU11 2BG *Monthly*

Soviet Weekly 3 Rosary Gardens, London SW7 4NW *Weekly*

Sport North The Editor, Sport North, Sports Council, County Court Building, Hallgarth Street, Durham DH1 3PB *Every four months*

Sunday Express Magazine (Unsold copies usually available from local newsagent) *Weekly*

Sunday Telegraph Magazine (Unsold copies usually available from local newsagent) *Weekly*

Sunday Times Magazine (Unsold copies usually available from local newsagent) *Weekly*

Talbot Times Talbot Times, International House, PO Box 712, Bickenhill Lane, Marston Green, Birmingham, West Midlands B37 7HZ *Monthly*

Telcom Today Marketing Executive, British Telecom, 2-12 Gresham Street, London WC2 *Monthly*

Tidy Times Keep Britain Tidy Group, Bostel House, 37 West Street, Brighton BN21 2RE *Quarterly*

TSB Family TSB Central Board, PO Box 33, Copthall Avenue, London EC2P 2AB *Three times a year*

The World's Children The Save the Children Fund, Jebb House, 157 Clapham Road, London SW9 0PT *Quarterly*

Young NSPCC News National Society for the Prevention of Cruelty to Children, Young League, 1 Riding House Street, London W1P 8AA *Quarterly*

Appendix 4

Sources of free 16mm films

The following list includes the main organizations which make films available, as well as distributors who act on behalf of some film sponsors. Addresses are given, as a considerable number are not readily available elsewhere. Where films can be obtained from more than one source, the principal source is given. All organizations issue lists or catalogues, the majority of which are free, from which it is possible to obtain basic details of individual titles.

Abbey National Building Society   27 Baker Street, London W1
Audience Planners   PO Box 44, Richmond, Surrey TW9 1UE
Australia—Agents—Generals   New South Wales, 66 Strand, London WC2; Queensland, 392-3 Strand, London WC2; South Australia, 50 Strand, London WC2; Western Australia, 115 Strand, London WC2; Victoria, Victoria House, Melbourne Place, London WC2
The Austrian Institute   28 Rutland Gate, London SW7 1PQ

Bahamas Tourist Office   Audience Planners, PO Box 44, Richmond upon Thames, Surrey TW9 1UE
Bahco Record Tools   Secretary-Sales and Marketing, Parkway Works, Sheffield S9 3BL
Barbados   Office of the High Commissioner for Barbados, 6 Upper Belgrave Street, London SW1X 8A2
Barclays Bank Ltd   Advertising Dept, Juxton House, 94 St Paul's Churchyard, London EC4M 8EH
British Petroleum   The BP Film Library, 15 Beaconsfield Road, London NW10 2LE
British Aerosol Manufacturers Association   Alembic House, 93 Albert Embankment, London SE1 7TU

Appendix 4

The British Insurance Association Aldermary House, Queen Street, London EC4N 1TU

British Sugar Bureau Film Library, 16 Paxton Place, London SE27 9SS

British Telecom British Telecom Film Library, 25 The Burroughs, London NW4 4AT

Brooke Bond Oxo Education Service Film Department, Leon House, High Street, Croydon CR9 1JQ

Cable and Wireless Ltd Public Relations Department, Mercury House, Theobalds Road, London WC1X 8RX. Films on modern Communication systems including use of satellites.

Canadian High Commission Film Library Canada House Film Library, Canada House, Trafalgar Square, London SW1Y 5BJ. Very comprehensive list of quality films on many general interest topics.

Civic Trust Information Recommended Films 17 Carlton House Terrace, London SW1Y 5AW. Films on the environment from 12 sources.

Concrete Society Publications Publications Distribution, Cement and Concrete Association, Wexham Springs, Slough SL3 6PL

CTVC Film Library, Foundation House, Walton Road, Bushey, Watford WD2 2JF

Danish Agricultural Producers 3 Conduit Street, London W1R 0AT

David Brown Tractors Ltd Meltham, Huddersfield HD7 3AR

EFVA National Audio Visual Aids Library, Paxton Place, Gipsy Road, London SE27 9SR

The Electricity Council Film Library, 15 Beaconsfield Road, London NW10 2LE

Forestry Commission Information Branch 231 Corstorphine Road, Edinburgh EH12 7AT

George Rowney & Co Ltd PO Box 10, Bracknell, Berkshire RG12 4ST

Ghana Office of the High Commission for Ghana, 13 Belgrave Square, London SW1X 8PR

Greece The National Tourist Organisation of Greece, 195-7 Regent Street, London W1R 8DL

Guild Sound and Vision Woodston House, Oundle Road, Peterborough PE2 9PZ. Catalogues available on each of the following subject areas:
1. Agriculture and farming 2. Civil engineering, construction and architecture 3. Commerce, business and careers 4. Domestic science 5. Electricity and electronics 6. Engineering, industry and mining 7. Manufacturing, mechanical handling and transport 8. Medical, first aid and accident prevention 9. Motoring and motorcycling 10. Social and education studies 11. Sport and recreation 12. Travel and places of interest — includes the following countries: Brazil, Denmark, Hungary, Isle of Man, Israel, Scotland.

Guyana Office of the High Commission for Guyana, 3 Palace Court, London W2 4LP

Hong Kong Government Information Services   6 Grafton Street, London W1X 3LB

Iceland Embassy   1 Eaton Terrace, London SW1W 8EY
India   The High Commission of India, Information Department, India House, Aldwych, London WC2B 4NA
Indonesian Embassy   Information Department, 38 Grosvenor Square, London W1X 9AD
The Italian Institute   39 Belgrave Square, London SW1X 8NX. Cultural films.
Italian State Tourist Office   Film Library, 1 Princes Street, London W1R 8AY

Japan Information Centre   Embassy of Japan, 9 Grosvenor Square, London W1X 9LB
JCB   Film Library Service, Swanlind Ltd, Wobaston Road, Fordhouses, Wolverhampton WV9 5HA

Kango Wolf Power Tools Ltd   Education Department, Wolf Electric Tools Ltd, Hanger Lane, London W5 1DS
Kenya High Commission   45 Portland Place, London W1N 4AS
Kodak Ltd   PO Box 66, Kodak House, Hemel Hempstead, Herts HP1 1JU

Lead Development Association   34 Berkeley Square, London W1X 6AJ

Malaysian High Commission   Information Department, Malaysian High Commission, 45 Belgrave Square, London SW1X 8QT
Midland Bank Film Library   Public Relations and Advertising Department, Griffen House, PO Box 2, 41 Silver Street, Sheffield S1 3EG

Neill Tools Ltd   Napier Street, Sheffield S11 8HB
New Zealand High Commission   Haymarket, London SW1. A wide range of interesting titles.

Pakistan   Embassy of Pakistan Information Division, 35 Lowndes Square, London W1
Phillips Petroleum Film Library   15 Beaconsfield Road, London NW10 1YD
P&O Group Library   Information and Public Relations, Beaufort House, St Botolph Street, London EC3A 7DK
Portuguese National Tourist Office   New Bond Street House, 1 New Bond Street, London W1

Random Film Library   25 The Burroughs, Hendon, London NW4 4AT. Films from Barclays Bank Ltd, Birds Eye Foods Ltd, British Telecom, Dunlop, Kodak, Lilia-White Sales Ltd, Quality Milk Producers Ltd, Whitbread & Co Ltd.
Rentokil   Rentokil Film Unit, Webber Road, Kirkby, Liverpool L33 7SR
Royal Danish Embassy   Press and Cultural Department, 55 Sloane Street, London SW1X 9SR

Appendix 4

Royal Norwegian Embassy   25 Belgrave Square, London SW1X 8QD

Scottish Central Film Library   Dowanhill, 74 Victoria Crescent Road, Glasgow G12 9JN
Scottish Tourist Board   23 Ravelston Terrace, Edinburgh EH4 3EU
Shell Film Library   25 The Burroughs, Hendon, London NW4 4AT
Singmaster, David   List of 16mm films on mathematical subjects. Polytechnic of the South Bank, Borough Road, London SE1 0AA
South African Embassy   Information Division, Trafalgar Square, London WC2N 5DP
The Spanish Institute   102 Eaton Square, London SW1 9AN (Membership £9 pa, then free)
Stanley Tools Ltd   Educational Service, Woodside, Sheffield S3 9PD
Swedish Embassy   Darvill Associates, 280 Chartridge Lane, Chesham, Bucks HP5 2SG

Thailand   Information Service of Thailand, 30 Queen's Gate, London SW7
Transport, travel and electricity film library   Melbury House, Melbury Terrace, London NW1 6LP
TSB   Group Central Executive   PO Box 33, 3 Copthall Avenue, London EC3P 2AB

Viscom Film and Video Library   Park Hall Road Trading Estate, London SE21 8EL. A major distributor of free films, including Barclays Bank, British Sugar Bureau, British Gas, UK Atomic Energy Authority, Elf Aquitaine, General Motors, Honda, RSPCA, Esso, Irish Tourist Board, Royal Mail, RNLI and German films.

Wadkin plc   Green Lane Works, Leicester LE5 4PF
Welsh Office Film Library   Crown Building, Cathays Park, Cardiff CF1 3NQ
Wedgwood and Coalport   Film Division, Press Office, Wedgwood Group, 34 Wigmore Street, London W1H 0HD

Yugoslavia National Tourist Office   143 Regent Street, London W1

Index

'*A' Level Economics Study Kit* 39
acquisition policy 126-127
advertisements, magazine 36
advertising 46
aerodromes, old 88
African studies 85
After the Arrow 35
agencies, government supported 22-23, 35
Agency Sources and Resources in the UK 73
Agricultural Chemicals and Wildlife 62
agriculture 49, 66, 81, 82, 103-108 *passim*
Agriculture, Ministry of 82, 104, 106
Agriculture and Fisheries for Scotland, Department of 81
Aims of Industry, The 45
Air — my enemy, The 67
aircraft illustrations 36, 37
Allinson Ltd 80
alternative energy sources 64, 65, 67, 71, 72
alternative information sources, directory of 12
alternative materials in libraries 12
'Alternatives' (*Guardian* series) 71
Alvis 37
Amateur Swimming Association 99
American studies 84
Amnesty International 101
animals 36, 37, 105, 106

Annual Careers Guide 49
annual reports
  firms' 36-37, 45
  UCCA's 49
apes: adjustment to ecological change 70
Archaeological Officers 87
archaeological societies 87
architecture
  advice for study of 32
  colour supplements 33
  films 36
armed forces: careers literature 52, 55
Army periodicals 52
art 30-37
  colleges 31
  colour supplements 32-34
  competitions 31
  films 34-36
  galleries/centres 31, 32, 33
  illustrations 36-37
  newspapers 34
  regional associations 31
art movements 33
artists 33, 35
Arts Council 31-32
  Bulletin 31
Arts in Action 31
Arts Review 31, 32
Aslib 129
Aspects of Secondary Education in England 6, 13
Association Engineers Ltd 125

Index

Association for the Conservation of
Energy 72
Association of Agriculture 82, 103-
104
Association of Certified Accountants
55
Association of British Ports 81
Association of Investment Trust
Companies 44
Association of Science Education
110
associations
publications of 12
teachers' professional 24, 85-86
athletics films 99
Atom 52, 72, 114, 117
atomic warfare 69
Australian Information Service 77
Austria, books on 84
Austrian Institute 90
automobile engineering 124
automobile industry periodical 52

Baltic Exchange 44
Bank Education Service 17, 28,
39-40, 95
Bank Reviews 40, 76, 81
banking 39-40
Barker, Ronnie 68
Basic Road Statistics 82
Bavaria, film on 96
BBC/Daily Mirror 17
BBC radio 28-29
Beauty in Trust 66
Beckmann, M 36
BEE 57-58
Beirut massacre 70
Below the Line 67
Best Western Hotels 18
Beswick, Barbara 8, 13, 14
Bevan, Ernest 69
bibliographies, historical 86-87
Bilharzia 66
birds 106, 114
Birmingham Museum and Art Gallery
32
Black Horse Guides 40
*BNFL at the Heart of Nuclear
Power* 67
Board of Inland Revenue 43
BOCM Silcock 106

Bonn, film on 96
book allowances: purchasing power
5
book fairs 128-129
booklets
banking 39
building societies 38
business 45-46
careers 48, 49, 50, 54-55, 56
commodities 44, 45
countries of the world 84
environmental studies 60, 61, 63
equipment leasing 44
farm stock management 106
higher education 49-50
housing 38
insurance 38, 41, 44
investment 38, 42, 44, 45
invisible exports 44
life assurance 42
metal trading 45
money 38, 39-40, 41
pension funds 45
religious studies 102
saving 38, 41
science 111-114 *passim*,
116-119 *passim*
ship chartering 44
small businesses 44
spark plugs and engines 124
sport 98-99
stock exchange 38, 42
takeovers and mergers 45
woodwork 120, 121, 122
books
agriculture 104
automobile engineering 124
average price of 5
careers 25, 46, 48, 49
countries of the world 84
environmental studies 58, 61-62
cookery 91, 93, 94
free 15-16, 20
general studies sourcebooks 72-74
jobs 50
science 111, 115
woodwork 120
Books for Schools 13
bookshops
school 128
specialist 12

Bosch, Hieronymus 36
Botanical Society of the British Isles
    63, 105
Bother 53
BP 115, 123
Brake, Terence 14
Brandt Report 71
Brazilian Indians: resistance to
    civilization 69
Brezhnev, Leonid Ilyich 69-70
Brice, Jennifer 8, 14
Britain 66, 67, 70, 81-82
Britain—an official handbook 27
Britain's Natural Gas 67
British Aerospace 37
British Agrochemical Association 107
British Association for the Advance-
    ment of Science 110-111
British Association of Young Scien-
    tists 110-111
British Banking System 40
British Council of Churches 101,
    102
British Diabetic Association 93
British Dietetic Association 93
British Economy in Figures 40
British Educational Equipment
    Association 6
British Eggs Authority 99
British Gas 67, 94
British Goat Society 106
British Home Stories 37
British Industrial and Sponsored
    Film Awards 19
British Insurance Association 41-42
British Insurance Brokers Associ-
    ation 44
British Isles 66, 69, 70, 81-82
British Library 9, 24
British Medical Association 74
British Museum 88, 89, 106
British Nuclear Forum 117
British Nutrition Foundation 91, 93
British Overseas Trade Board 43-44
British Petroleum 115, 123
British Ports Authority 88
British Road Federation 16, 62, 82
British Safety Council 93
British Shipping News 76
British Society for Social Responsi-
    bility in Science 110

British Standards Institution 16, 93
British Telecom 17, 114, 118-119
British Telecom Journal 52
British Tourist Authority 81
British Waterways Board 88
British Wool Marketing Board 19,
    108
Broadsheets 71
brochures 36, 42
Brown (David) Tractors 125
BSA Bulletin 39
building societies 38-39
*Building Societies and House
    Purchase* 38
Building Societies Association 39
Building Societies: study folder 38
Building Society News 39
buildings
    ancient 32, 90
    subterranean 70
Bulletin of Environmental Education
    57, 58
bulletins, art 31
Burmah 125
buses, history of 55, 88
business studies 37-46
*Buying a House on an Option
    Mortgage* 39

Cable and Wireless Ltd 119
Caledonian Pipeline 67
calendars available locally 15
Campaign Books 12, 14
'Canada at war' series 89
Canada House 99-100
canals 88, 90
card indexes 126-127, 129
careers 16, 25, 46-56
    booklets 48, 49, 50, 54-55
    books 25, 46, 48, 49
    card index of jobs by interest areas
        48
    dual purpose of literature 56
    films 48, 53-54
    insurance 41
    leaflets 48, 54-56
    literature acquired and organized
        by students 56
    local authority careers service 47
    newspapers 51, 53
    periodicals 47, 50-53

Index

careers (cont)
  school policy 47
Careers and Occupational
  Information
    Centre 47-50 *passim*, 53
Careers Encyclopedia 25, 46, 50
Careers Library Classification Index
  48
Careers Research and Advisory
  Centre 50, 51
caricatures 33
Carters Seeds 107
cartoon films 36
Case History — Redcar and Coldrife
  67
Cashew Nut 78
Cassell's *Careers Encyclopedia* 25,
  46, 50
Castrol 108, 112-113, 125
Catalogue of Careers Films 53
Catalogues of Art Exhibitions 32
Catch, The 68
cataloguing 127
Central Electricity Generating Board
  66, 67
Central Film Library 22, 35, 68, 90,
  124
central government... *see* govern-
  ment...
Central Hinterland 77
Central Office of Information 21,
  22, 79, 81
Central Register and Clearing House
  Ltd 49
Central Services Unit for Univer-
  sities and Polytechnics Careers
  and Appointments Services 50
Centre for World Development
  Education 26, 73, 79
Certificate of Secondary Education
  farm machinery 107-108
  geography 16
  history 86
Champion spark plugs 124
Changing Food Habits in the UK 63
Changing Forest, The 66
charges for firms' material 28
charities 25, 31, 101-102
Charities Digest 25
Chemical Industries Association 111
chemical industry 111-112, 115-117

chemical warfare 69
cheques 17, 40
child care 93
Chile: internal conflict 70
China: juvenile delinquency 69
China Reconstructs 72, 75
Chirico, Giorgio de 33
Choice, The 66
Christian Aid 102
Christian Education Movement
  101, 102-103
Church Missionary Society 103
Church of England Children's
  Society 25, 101
churches 87-88
Civic Trust 32, 61, 87
Civil Service 54-55
*Classified Guide to Sources of
  Educational Film Material* 76
Claymore Story, The 10
colour supplements
  art 32-34
  available locally 15
  value of material from 9
colours for artists, films on 35
commerce 37-46
Commission for Racial Equality 16, 28
  periodical 72
  poster competition 31
Commission of the European
  Communities 65, 71-72
Committee of Directors of Poly-
  technics 51
Committee of the Churches 101
Committee on Invisible Exports 44
commodities 44, 45, 80-81
Common Market 65, 71-72, 75,
  79-80, 84
*Commonwealth: a guide to material
  and information services available to schools and to the public*
  22, 78-79
Commonwealth Institute 80
communication 27, 118
community enterprises 71
Community Information Project 9
Community Service Volunteers 62
companies *see* firms
*Compendium of Advanced Courses
  in Colleges of Further and Higher
  Education* 49

Index

Compendium of Information for Entrance 49
computers and individual privacy 71
Confederation of British Industry 9
CONOCO 90
Conservation News 59
Conservation Society 26, 59
Conservation Trust 58, 59, 60, 80
Constable, John 33
Constructurists Group 33
Consumer News 92
cookery 91, 93-94
COSIRA 44
costume
  films 36
  postcards 32
  wallchart 88
cottages 33
Council for Education in World Citizenship 26, 71, 73, 75, 79
Council for Educational Technology 10
Council for Environmental Education 26, 59-60, 61, 65, 76, 80
Council for National Academic Awards 49
Council for Nature 63, 105
Council for Small Industries in Rural Areas 44
Council of Subject Teaching Association 24
councils, local *see* local authorities
countries
  bank reviews 40, 76, 81
  books and booklets 84
  information centres 84-85
  maps 18
  source books 26, 78-80
countryside 105-106
Countryside Commission 105
County Archaeological Societies 87
County Naturalist Trust 31
County Record Office 87
Courtaulds 117
CRAC 50
Cranach, Lucas 36
Cryla 35
Cubism 33
cultivation 106-107
currency of low-cost resources 28-29, 126

Curriculum Decision-making and Educational Television 16, 20

Daily Telegraph 28, 50, 53
Dairy Education News 76
dairy products 76, 108
Dairylea 89
dancing, films on 99
David, John 20
defence 72, 76
Defence, Ministry of 55, 88
degree course leaflets 49
dental care 93
Department of . . . *see subject area covered*, eg Education and Science, Department of
Design Council 92
design technology films 124
detergents 95
Development Commission 44
Development Guide, The 73
Development News 53, 72, 76
dietetics 93, 95
Directory of Environmental Literature and Teaching Aids 60, 65
Directory of First Degree and Diploma of Higher Education Courses 49
Directory of Pressure Groups 26
Directory of Resource Materials for Teachers of Technology in Schools, 1976 110, 123
documentaries: newspaper synopses 71
Drabble, Phil 67
drawing, films on 35
drug problem in United States 69
Dunlop 81
Durer, Albrecht 33, 35, 36
Durham, Mike 13

Earth Science Conservation 76
East/West relations 69-70
Economic Association 45
economic geography 76
economic growth 71
Economic Profile of Britain 40
Economic Progress Report 72, 92
Economic Transition, The 59
economics 37-46, 71, 72, 81

economics (cont)
'A' Level study kit   39
bank reviews   40, 76, 81
Economist, The   45
Ecosocialism in a Nutshell   64
Education and Science, Department
    of   5-6, 10, 13, 14, 15, 20, 22,
    49, 60, 72-73, 79
Education Committee Year Book   24
education departments
    firms'   28
    nationalized industries'   27
    pressure groups'   26
Educational and Television Films Ltd
    36, 77
Educational Foundation for Visual
    Aids   35, 76
educational kits   19
educational methods, factors affecting
    7
educational press   28
Educational Publishers Council   5, 6,
    13, 129
Egg Machine   66
electricity   94, 117-118
Electricity Council   94, 117
embassies   18, 26, 29, 36, 78, 83
employers' organizations   55
Employment, Department of   51
Employment News   51, 72
Encyclopedia Britannica   35
Energen Food Company   94
energy
    alternatives   64, 65, 67, 71, 72
    environmental sources   63, 64,
    66-67
    nationalized industries   27, 82, 94
    periodicals   52-53, 65, 72, 112-113
    power supply industries   82, 94
Energy in Perspective   67
Energy—the Nuclear Option   67
Energy to Use or Abuse   16, 20
engineering periodicals   52
Environment, Department of   39, 61,
    62, 65, 87
Environment and the Community
    61-62
Environment in the Balance   65
Environmental Education   57
Environmental Education Enquiries
    60

Environmental Group Information
    Service   63
environmental information sources
    26, 32
environmental studies   56-68
    booklets   60, 61, 63
    books   58, 61-62
    course planning   57
    films   65-68
    leaflets   62
    organizations   57-61
    periodicals   57, 61, 62-63, 64-65,
    76
    political theory involvement   64
    teachers' guides   59
Epstein, Jacob   35
Equipment Leasing Association   44
Eritrea   69
Esso Magazine   52-53, 72, 76, 113
Esso Petroleum   115, 125
Ethnic Minorities in Britain   16
Euroforum   65, 71-72
*Europe Information External
    Relations* periodicals   72
Europe '82   72, 75
European Commission   64
European Community   71, 75
*European Community—a brief
    reading list*   79
*European Community Information
    Series—a guide to the literature
    and an indication of sources of
    information*   79
European Community Publications
    80
European Court of Human
    Rights   70
European Documentation
    Centres   84
European Economic Community *see*
    Common Market
European Environment 1975—2000
    59
Eurostat News   75
exhibitions
    art   32, 34
    home economics material from   91
Exley Publications   12
expenditure on library books   5-6, 13
exports   43-44

Index

fabric care   94, 95
facsimile manuscripts   89
fact sheets
  Central Office of Information   81
  religious   101
Facts About Building Societies   38
Facts About Business   45
Family magazine   40
Family Welfare Association   25
farming 49, 66, 81, 82, 103-108
  passim
  machinery   107-108
fashion
  history   88
  illustrations   37
  museum   33
Fashion Through the Ages AD950 —
  1937   88
fauna and flora   36, 37, 62-63,
  105-106
Fauna Preservation Society   63
Federation of Commodity Associations   44
Feed the minds   102
fertilizers   66, 106-107
Fibre Building Board Development
  Association   121
fiction, promotion of   129
Film Board of Canada   19
films   19, 29, 146-149
  art   34-36
  building societies   39
  business and economics   46
  careers   48, 53-54
  Christian Church   103
  environmental studies   65-68
  farm machinery   108
  film shows   128
  from embassies   27
  from nationalized industries   27
  geography   76-78
  Germany   96-97
  history   89-90
  home economics   95
  insurance   41
  libraries   19, 27, 34-36, 54, 89,
    96, 97, 99, 100, 118
  posters   36
  science   110, 114-119 *passim*
  sport   99-100
  stock exchange   43

films (cont)
  tools   120-121, 124-125
filmstrips from nationalized industries
  27
Finance Houses Association   45
financial documents   17
Financial Times   28, 83
firms   15, 27-28, 29, 82
  annual reports   36-37, 45
  art competitions   31
  commodity dealers   80-81
  home economics publications   94
  multinational   56, 65-66, 77
  nationalized industries   27
  products   36-37
  small businesses   44
  visual historical material   89
First Look at Oil, A   16
First World War (films)   90
Fisons   106-107
Fissile Society, The   63
flight, history of (film)   90
flowers   36, 63, 105
Focus   51
food   63-64, 91-95 *passim*
football (film)   99
Forbes Publications Ltd   91
Ford News   52
Foreign and Commonwealth Office
  53
forestry   49, 66, 82, 105, 121, 122
Forestry Commission   23, 66, 82,
  105, 121, 122
forms   17, 43
Forum Council of Europe   72
Foundations of Wealth   46
Free Stuff for Kids   12
French language   97
Friedrich, Caspar David   36
Friends of the Earth   63
fuels industries   82, 94
'Futures, the world of science and
  technology' (*Guardian* series)
  70-71

gardening   49, 106-107
gas   67, 118
Gas Council   66
General Dental Council   93
general studies and contemporary
  problems   68-74

general studies and contemporary
   problems (cont)
   newspapers   68-71
   periodicals   71-72
   source books   72-74
*Geographer's Vademecum of Sources
   and Materials, The*   78
Geographical Association   24
geography   74-85
   British Isles   81-82
   Certificate of Secondary Education
      16
   commodities   44, 45, 80-81
   countries of the world   82-85
   films   76-78
   periodicals   75-76
   source books   78-80
German Institute   96
German language   96-97
Goethe Institute   96
Golden Films   54
golf films   100
Good Earth   59
Good Neighbours   67
government departments   21-22,
   35-36, 78, 113-114
government policy effects (Britain)
   70
government publications on home
   economics   92
government supported agencies
   22-23, 35
grants for students   49, 51
Grants to Students:a brief guide   49
Grassroots Books   12, 14
Green, Anthony   33
Green Alliance   64
Grierson, John   19
Guardian, The   65, 70-71, 83
*Guide to Agency Sources and
   Resources in the UK*   79
*Guide to Resources in Environ-
   mental Education*   58
Guild Sound and Vision   77, 90,
   100, 124-125
Gundrey, Elizabeth   12
gymnastics films   99

hardboard   121-122
Harvest   67
Hazards Bulletin   110

Health Education Council   91, 93,
   129
Hepworth, Barbara   35
herbicides   66
Heritage Education Group   61
Heseltine, Michael   70
higher education: low-cost printed
   sources   49-50, 51
Highlands and Islands Development
   Board   44
Hill, Rowland   88
hill walking film   100
hire purchase agreements   17
Hiroshima   69
Historic Buildings Council   32
Historical Association   24, 85-86
history   85-90
History of Malta, The   89
History of the Mail, The   17
HMSO   21, 92, 106
Hockney, David   33
Holbein, Hans   36
Holland, Philip   23
home economics   90-95
   leaflets   16
horses, illustrations of   36, 37
horticulture   49, 106-107
hotel maps   18
household finance   95
housing   38
Housing Facts   38
How Life Insurance Works   42
*How to Apply for Admission to
   University*   49
How to Use a Cheque   40
Hydrological System, The   17

ICI   28, 66, 107, 115-116
Impressionists, Early   33
income tax   17, 43
Independent Broadcasting Authority
   15, 20
India Documentary Films   78
industrial firms *see* firms
Industrial Training Boards   50, 55
Industry, Department of   44, 111
Industry/Education View   113-114
*Information in the Secondary
   School Curricula*   9, 14
Information Services in Education
   24

Index

Inland Revenue   43
Innovation and Research in Education   14
Institute of Petroleum   16
Institute of Practitioners in Advertising   46
Institute of Public Relations   28, 78
insurance   38, 41-42, 44
internal combustion engine   90, 123-124
international environment   63-64
International Understanding: sources of information on international organizations—a handbook for schools and colleges   15, 20, 22, 72-73, 79, 85
investment   38, 42, 44, 45
invisible exports   44
Iran/Iraq war   70
Irish history (film)   89
iron and steel industries   27
Iron in Western Australia   77
Issuing Houses Association   44

Japan Pictorial   75
Japanese firms in Wales   69
Jellicoe, Sir Geoffrey   33
jobs: low-cost printed sources   50
John Deere News   72
judo films   100
juvenile delinquency in China   69

Kandinsky, Vasily   36
Keesings Archives   68
Kelly's Directories   27, 36
Kent-Barlow Information Associates   129
King, David   14
kits   19
Klee, Paul   36
Kobell, F   36
Kruger National Park   68

Lamp Project   111
Land Area Usage Figures   81
Land Must Provide, The   66
Last, Derick   10, 14
Latin-American studies   85
Lawn Tennis Association   99
leaflets   16
  art illustrations   36

leaflets (cont)
  careers   48, 54-56
  countries of the world   83-84
  degree and other advanced courses   49
  environment studies   62
  farm machinery   107-108
  history   86
  home economics   16
  income tax   43
  insurance   41
  science   116, 117
leasing, equipment   44
Leonard, Michael   33
Lever Bros   94, 95
Librarians for Social Change   12, 14
libraries
  film   19, 27, 34-36, 54, 89, 96, 97, 99, 100, 118
  links between local and school libraries   12
  see also school libraries
library resource centres, growth of   7
life assurance   42
Life Cycle of Water   17
Life in the Balance   66
Life Offices Association   42
listed buildings   32
Living Pattern, The   66
Living with Gas   67
Lloyds Bank   40
local authorities
  careers services   47
  publications from   44
  sources of primary material   23-24
local media   29
Local Studies Collections   86-87
London Boroughs Association Handbook   44
London Commodity Exchange   45
London Diplomatic List, The   78, 83
London Discount Market Association   45
London: facts and figures   44
London Metal Exchange   45
Longworth, Norman   9, 14
Look to the Hills   66
Look to the Land   66
Love and Sex—feelings in relationships   17

low-cost material, value of 8-11
Lowry, L S 34
lubricating oil 125
Lucky Child? Unlucky Child? 5, 13
Luncheon Voucher Catering
    Education Research Institute 91
Lyons Tetley 80, 81

Mackintosh, Charles Rennie 33
Magic of the Rails 78
mailing lists 28
Malta, history of (film) 89
Manet, Edouard 33
man-made fibres 117
manuscript facsimiles 89
maps 18, 87, 97
Margin of Averages 41
Matthews, Peter 13
media and politics 69
mergers 45
metal trading 45
metalwork 122-125
Metropolitan Line 88
microcomputers 129
microfilming 87
Midland Bank
    town plans 18
    wallcharts 17
Miss Selfridge 37
modern languages 96-97
Monet, Claude 33
money 38, 39-40, 41
Money and You 42
Money in the Community 17
money management 37-46
Money Saving and Investment 17
Monsanto 117
Moray House College of Education
    8
Morby, G 14
motor industry 52, 112-115 *passim*,
    123-124
motor racing history 90
multinational firms
    careers literature 56
    films 65-66, 77
Municipal Year Book 24
Murphy Chemical 107
museums
    art facilities 31, 32, 36
    fashion 33

museums (cont)
    historical resources 87, 88
    My Word is My Bond 43

Nagasaki 69
National Association for Environ-
    mental Education 57, 72, 106
National Association for Maternal
    and Child Welfare 92, 93
National Association of Pension
    Funds 45
National Book League 5, 6, 13
National Bus Company 55, 82, 88
National Centre for Alternative
    Technology 64
National Centre for School Tech-
    nology 110
National Centre for Science and
    Technology 114, 123
National Children's Bureau 92
National Christian Education Move-
    ment 103
National Coal Board 67
National Committee for Audio-Visual
    Aids in Education 76
National Consultative Committee for
    Agricultural Education 49
National Council of Social Service
    25
National Dairy Council 29, 91, 108
National Farmers Union 66
National Federation of Young
    Farmers Clubs 106
National Gallery 32
National Health Service 69
National Marriage Council 92
National Parks 105
national savings 38, 41, 88
National Savings Committee 41, 88
National Trust 66, 105
    houses 33
National Union of Teachers 8
National Water Council 17
National Westminster Bank 40
nationalized indsustries 27, 82
    careers literature 55
    poster competitions 31
    visual historical material 88
NATO 16
NATO Review 72, 76
natural history films 67

Index

Naturalist Trusts 105
Nature Conservancy Council 62, 66, 76
Nature Newsletter 63
Naturopa 62-63
Navy
  periodicals 52
  Russian 70
Need to Know project 9, 14
Netherlands: map of recently reclaimed areas 18
New Equals 72
New Town Association 81
New Zealand Film Library 100
Newscheck 47, 50, 53
newsletters
  charities' 25
  environmental studies 58
newspapers
  art competitions 31
  arts articles 34
  available locally 15
  careers 51, 53
  countries of the world 83
  educational 28
  general studies 68-71
  quality 28-29
  regions of the UK 81-82
  value of material from 9
  see also colour supplements
Nightingale, Florence 88
North West Water Authority 17
nuclear energy 52, 67, 117
Nuclear Generation 67
Nuclear Prospects 63
nuclear war 69, 70
Nuremburg 33

Observer, The 53, 65, 69-70
'Observers' books 37
Occidental Oil 10
Office of Fair Trading 16
Office of Population Census and Survey 18
oil industry 52-53, 64, 65-66, 77, 112-113, 114-115
old buildings, preservation of 69, 90
Old Masters, postcards of 32
One Day 38
opinion polls 70

organization of material 127-128
organizations, local 12
Oriental and African studies 85
overseas development 26
Overseas Development, Minister of 22
Overseas Development Administration 72, 76
Overseas Development and Aid 22, 73, 79
Overseas Development Institute 73
overseas trade 43-44
Oxfam 25, 28, 53, 64, 71, 101-102

painters and paintings
  colour supplements on 32-34
  films on 35
Pakistan, book on 84
pamphlets 16
  consumer economy and the environment 64
  countryside 105-106
  history 86
Panel on Takeovers and Mergers 45
Parkinson, Norman 34
Pasternak, Leonid 37
PAYE 43
Pedigree Petfoods 37
Peel, Harold 7, 14
pension funds 45
People and Season 66
People in Britain 18
periodicals 17, 25, 27, 142-145
  armed forces 52
  art 31-32
  building societies 39
  careers 47, 50-53
  energy 65, 72
  engineering 52
  environmental studies 57, 61, 62-63, 64-65
  general studies 71-72
  geography 75-76
  history 85
  home economics 91
  money management 42
  motor industry 112-113
  oil industry 52-53, 112-113
  overseas trade 43
  physical education 98

Index

periodicals (cont)
  religion 101
  rural studies 104, 108
  Russian satirical 33
  science 110, 111, 112-114
  sport 98
  stock exchange 42-43
  Voluntary Services Overseas 53
  woodwork 121
  workshop technology 123
Perkins Engines 123
pesticides 66, 107
Pesticides in Focus 66
pets 37, 106
PETT 54
Philishave 99
Phillips Petroleum 110
photocopies of popular objects 37
photocopying
  illegal 7
  permission to copy wallcharts 18
photographs of art subjects 37
photography 34, 35
Photoposters 48
physical education 97-100
  Association 97-98
Pictorial Discussion Sheets 64
picture loan collections 31
Picture Post (film) 35
Pigments to Palette 35
Pinochet Ugarte, General Augusto 70
Planning Your Environment 62
Poland, unrest in 69
political theory and environmental education 64
politics
  alternative agenda 71
  media and 69
Politics of Urban Transport Planning 63
pollution 59, 61, 63, 64, 66, 67
Polytechnic of North London 16, 111
Pony 36, 37
Pope John Paul II 69
population 64
ports authorities 82, 88
Post Office 17, 18, 88
  films 35
  poster competitions 31

postage stamps 35, 88
postcards 18
  art 32, 36
  British birds 106
  historical 88
posters 18, 27
  art illustrations 36
  careers classification 48
  careers information 48
  communications 118
  competitions 31
  countries of the world 84
  endangered flora and fauna 63
  engines 123
  fashion 37
  films 36
  France 97
  Germany 97
  history 88
  rare British plants and creatures 105
  science 114, 117-118
  sport 99
  woodwork 120
poverty 64
power supply industries 82, 94
prehistoric life 88, 89
Pre-Raphaelites, postcards of drawings by 32
preserving old buildings 69
press, educational 28
pressure groups 25, 26, 59
Prestel 129
primitive art, films on 36
Printed Photographic Display Material 21
Procter and Gamble 95
product institutes 24-25
professional associations 24-25
  careers literature 55-56
  teachers' 24, 85-86
Project 52, 113
Project Engineers and Technology for Tomorrow 54
promotion of the library 128-129
prospectuses, higher education 50
public bodies: careers literature 54-55
public corporations 27
public libraries
  Local Studies Collection 86-87

Index

public libraries (cont)
  picture loan collections 31
  spending on books 6
public relations 28, 29
public utilities 23-24, 82, 94
publicity literature 129
Publishing for Schools 13
puppetry, films on 36
purchasing power of book allowances 5

Quangos: a definitive survey 23

racial equality 72
racquet sports 100
Raddon, Rosemary 8, 14
radio 28-29
  local 31, 87
  newspapers synopses of documentaries 71
railway, Indian (Dandakaranya) 78
Rainbow Verdict, The 35
raw materials 19
Record Ridgway 120
Regional Advisory Councils 49
Regional Art Associations 31
Regional Co-ordination of Educational Technology Arrangements, The 10
regional exploitation of resources 10
regional offices
  government agencies 23
  public utilities 23-24
regions, UK 66, 81-82
Register of Members of the Institute of Public Relations 27-28, 78
religious education 100-103
Rembrandt 35
Representative Associations and Directory of British Associations and Associations in Ireland 26
Research for Power 67
Research Machines RML 380Z microcomputer 129
resource centre growth 7
Resource Directories of Local Industry—a guide to their compilation 112
'Resource Sheets' for environmental studies 60-61

resources available in and around school 15
Restoration of Land after Open Cast Coalmining 67
Rethink—a course or a job or both? 51-52
Review of Environmental Education 61
Review of External Trade Statistics 43
RHM Foods 94
RIBA Directory of Films 54
Richardson, Nigel 9, 14
Risk Takers, The 41
River Must Live, The 66
river pollution 66
roads 82, 90
Robinsons 89
Rogers, Rick 14
Role of the Building Societies, The 38
Roman Britain 88
Rowney, George, and Company Ltd 35
Royal Academy Summer Exhibition (1975) 32
Royal Airforce Film Library 100
Royal Institute of British Architects 32, 54
Royal Institute of Chartered Surveyors 55
Royal Mail Film Library 100
Royal National Lifeboat Institution 101
Royal Society for the Prevention of Accidents 93
Royal Society for the Prevention of Cruelty to Animals 66, 106
Rubbish Tips 68
rugby 99, 100
Rugby Union 99
rural environment 62-63
rural studies 103-109
Russia
  naval strength 70
  periodical 72, 75
  relations with the West 69-70
'Russian Satirical Journals': colour supplement 33

safety at home 93

Index

Sales List of Reference Documents
  21, 81
Salisbury Cathedral spire: colour
  supplement   33
samples
  of banking stationery   39
  of materials   19
  of products   25
Sam's Song   39
Satellite Communication   17
Save the Children   72, 101, 102
saving, booklets on   38, 41, 42
Savings Facts   38
Savings Wise   42
Scala   75, 97
school bookshops   128
School Curriculum   10, 14
School Information Retrieval   129
school libraries
  acquisition policy   126-127
  careers information provision   47
  cost effectiveness   12
  growth of resource centres   7
  organization of material   127-128
  promotion of the library   128-129
  provision of alternative materials 12
School Natural Science Society   110,
  111
School Technology   114
schools, book provision in   5-6
Schools Information Centre on the
  Chemical Industry   109, 111-112
*Schools Liaison Questions and
  Answers*   115
science   109-119
science and technology, *Guardian*
  series on 70-71
Science for People   110
Science Museum   108
Scottish Colleges of Agriculture   104
Scottish Council for Technology   22
Scottish Film Library   22, 34
Scottish universities   49
sculpture films   35, 36
Search for Solutions   110
Seas Around Us, The   67
Second World War (films)   89-90
Sectional Lists   21, 23
See Haryana   78
*Semi Conductors and the Silicon
  Chip*   16

Service de Documentation Péda-
  gogique   97
Service du Cinéma   97
service organizations   25
*Services Available to the United
  Kingdom Public*   21
sex education films   95
Shell   16, 20, 28, 52-53, 64, 65, 66,
  90, 105, 107, 114-115, 125
Shell Education News   113
Shelter   25
Sheridan, Duffy: colour supplement
  33
ship chartering   44
Signposts   48
Singapore High Commission   16, 20
Singapore '82   16, 20
SIR   129
Small Firms Information Service   44
Smith, W H   128
Social Services Year Book   25
Socialist Environment and Resources
  Association   64
societies
  archaeological   87
  publications of   12, 87
Society for Education through Art
  32
Society for the Protection of Ancient
  Buildings   32
Soil Association   107
Solid Fuel Advisory Board   94
Something to Sing About   66
*Source Book for Agriculture Edu-
  cation*   8
*Source Book of Visual Aids Materials
  for the Teaching of Commerce* 8
source books
  general studies   72-74
  geography   78-80
  home economics   91
  rural studies   103-104
  science   109-110
*Sources of Information on Inter-
  national Organizations*   73, 79
sources of materials   21-29
*Sources of Teaching Aids and
  Facilities for Teachers of the
  Science and Technology of
  Catering, Home Economics and
  Related Subjects*   91

Index

South African spying 69
Southern Regional Council for
  Further Education 8
Soviet Weekly 72, 75
speakers
  from local organizations 29
  from nationalized industries 27
  on architecture 32
  on banking 40
  on building societies 39
  on history 87
  on insurance 41-42
special interest groups 25-26
Special Reports 83
spending on library books 5-6
sponsorship of art competitions 31
*Sponsorships and Supplementary
  Awards* 48
Sports Council 98
Spot the Difference 68
spying, South African 69
Square Deal, The 41
stamps 35, 88
Standard Telephones and Cables
  Ltd 119
Stanley Tools Ltd 18, 120-121
statistics
  embassies as sources of 26
  non-official sources 10-11
  overseas trade 43
  Scottish agriculture 81
Sterling, Stephen 57
stock exchange
  booklets 38, 42
  film 43
  periodical 42-43
Story of British Insurance, The 16
Strongest Link, The 39
study packs/kits
  'A' Level economics 39
  building societies 38-39
  insurance 41
Summary for Districts 81
Sunday Telegraph, The 70
Sunday Times, The 65, 69, 89
'Surrealism: Giorgio de Chirico':
  colour supplement 33
Surridge, Owen 13
survival in an inhospitable world 70
swimming 99
synthetic fibres 117

takeovers 45
Talbot, William Henry Fox: colour
  supplement 34
Tate and Lyle 80
taxation 43
Taylor Woodrow 99
teacher education courses 49
teachers' centre, art groups based at
  31
teachers' professional associations
  24, 85-86
Teachers' Handbook 82
Teaching Aids (British Insurance
  Association) 41
Teaching Aids (Building Societies
  Association) 38
teaching aids
  history 86
  international environment 63-64
Teaching History 85
technical studies 119-125
teeth, care of 93
telecommunications periodicals 52,
  114
telephone directories 24, 27
television
  children's art competitions 31
  newspaper synopses of docu-
    mentaries 71
tennis 99, 100
textile industry, Indian 78
Third World 26, 64, 71, 72, 73-74,
  101-102
Thomas, Harford 71
Thorpe, Stephen 9, 14
Threat in the Water, The 66
Timber Research and Development
  Association 19, 121
Times, The 83
Times Educational Supplement 28
To Live Like a Pig 66
Tomorrow's Coal 67
Too Good to Waste 67
tools 120-121, 124-125
tourist offices 26-27, 81, 87
Tower of London (film) 90
Town and Country Planning
  Association 26, 57-58, 80
town plans 18
trade, overseas 43-44
trade associations 24-25

Index

Trades Union Congress 46
transport 63, 65
  films 90, 97
  illustrations 36, 37, 89
  nationalized industries 27, 82
Transport and Travel Film Library 97
Transworld International 100
Treasure Chest for Teachers 8, 25, 28, 78
Treasures of Ireland 89
trees 49, 66, 82, 105, 121, 122
Trobridge, Ernest George: colour supplement 33
Trustee Savings Bank 40
Turner, Joseph Mallord William: colour supplement 33
Types of Farming in Britain 104
types of materials 15-20

UCCA 49
Understanding British Industry Project 9, 14, 28, 50, 56
Understanding Electricity 94, 117
unemployment 72
UNICEF 74, 102
Unilever 45, 116
Unit Trust Association 45
United Kingdom Atomic Energy Authority 52, 114, 117
United Nations Food and Agriculture Organization 80
United Society for the Propagation of the Gospel 103
United States, drug problem in 69
Universities Central Council on Admissions 49
university courses 49-50
University of Manchester Department of Town and Country Planning 65
Urban and Environmental Studies: a film guide 65
urban environment 61-62, 68
Useful Addresses for Science Teachers 8, 109
Using the Coal 67
Using the Local Environment 59

value of low-cost material 8-11

'Vatican Spectacular': colour supplement 33
vegetable gene bank 71
Vegetable Protein Association 93
Vegetarian Society of the United Kingdom 93
Victoria and Albert Museum 32
Victorians, The 88
videocassette films 115, 117, 118, 120
villages: film 90
Viscom Film Library 54, 118
Voluntary Services Overseas 53
Voluntary Social Services Handbook 25

Wales, Japanese firms in 69
Walesa, Lech 69
wallcharts 17-18
  banking 39-40
  dairy products 108
  farm machinery 108
  from nationalized industries 27
  history 88, 89
  home economics 95
  life assurance 42
  maps of Germany 97
  rural environment 62
  science 114-117 *passim*
  woodwork 120, 121-122
  workshop technology 123, 124
War on Want 102
war strategies 72
washing clothes 94, 95
Wastage in the UK Food System 63
water 64, 82
Water Council 82
Way with Weeds, A 66
weapons, illustrations of 36, 37
Weave Me Some Flowers 78
Welsh Development Agency 44
Welsh Film Library 22
Welsh Office 28
Wesfarmers — working for the man on the land 77
West German Film Library 36, 89, 96, 99
Western Australia Catalogue 77
Western Freightway 77
Westland Helicopters 37

Index

What Advertising Does 46
What Goes on in the City 40
What is Life Assurance 42
Where Rubber Begins 81
Which Course? 51, 52
Whitaker's Almanack 22-23, 27, 74, 78
White Fish Authority 74
Wild are Free, The 68
wildlife conservation 67-68
woodwork 120-122
word processing 71
worksheets 17
workshop technology 122-125
World Council of Churches 101, 102
World Economic Comment 43

World Studies Resource Guide 26, 73, 79
World Wildlife Fund 63
World's Children, The 72
Wragg, Professor E C 7, 13
Wyperfield 68

You and Your Rights 17
Young, Michael 7, 14
Youth Environmental Action 62

Zola, Emile: colour supplement 34

250 More Things to Send Off For 12
2,000 Years of Houses 38
10,000 Years of Money 38